Raspberry Pi LED Blueprints

Design, build, and test LED-based projects using Raspberry Pi

Agus Kurniawan

BIRMINGHAM - MUMBAI

Raspberry Pi LED Blueprints

First published: September 2015

Production reference: 1210915

Published by Packt Publishing Ltd.
Livery Place
35 Livery Street
Birmingham B3 2PB, UK.

ISBN 978-1-78217-575-9

www.packtpub.com

Credits

Author
Agus Kurniawan

Reviewers
David Alcoba

Parul Sharma

Commissioning Editor
Neil Alexander

Acquisition Editor
Vivek Anantharaman

Content Development Editor
Aparna Mitra

Technical Editor
Tejaswita Karvir

Copy Editor
Dipti Mankame

Project Coordinator
Izzat Contractor

Proofreader
Safis Editing

Indexer
Hemangini Bari

Graphics
Jason Montciro

Production Coordinator
Shantanu N. Zagade

Cover Work
Shantanu N. Zagade

About the Author

Agus Kurniawan is a lecturer, IT consultant, and author. He has experience in various software and hardware development projects, delivering materials in training and workshops, and delivering technical writing for 14 years. He has been awarded the Microsoft Most Valuable Professional (MVP) award for 11 years in a row.

He is currently doing some research and teaching activities related to networking and security systems at the Faculty of Computer Science, University of Indonesia, and Samsung R&D Institute, Indonesia. Currently, he is pursuing a PhD in computer science in Germany. He can be reached on his blog at http://blog.aguskurniawan.net, and Twitter at @agusk2010.

First, I am thankful to the entire team at Packt, especially Vivek, Aparna, Tejaswita, and the reviewers, for being so cooperative and patient with me. They have been a great help, and their feedback and hints have improved the manuscript considerably.

This book is dedicated to all open source makers, developers, contributors, and enthusiasts from Raspberry Pi communities.

I would like to thank my wife, Ela Juitasari, my son, Thariq, and daughter, Zahra, for their support and encouragement.

About the Reviewers

David Alcoba, for many years, has been working as a software engineer, who likes to play with electronics in his spare time. While he was responsible for designing and building highly secure distributed applications for the industry, he also decided to start gaining more and more knowledge of digital fabrication tools every day. Then, he realized that he'd just discovered a world where all of his different interests could be merged into a single project.

Based on this idea, he helped create Vailets Hacklab in 2014, a local community in Barcelona that aims to hack the current educational system so that kids might become cocreators of their future through technology instead of being just consumers.

Following the spirit of this initiative, David decided to cofound Makerkids Barcelona, a small start-up focused on providing professional services for schools and organizations to engage kids into the new maker movement and follow the STEAM (science, technology, engineering, art, and mathematics) educative principles.

Parul Sharma is a commissioning engineer. He has experience in project erection and commissioning, robotics, and hardware hacking. He has a good skill set of programming languages. He also works as a freelancer for developing and mentoring projects for engineering students. He has expertise in LabVIEW, SIMATIC, TIA, and Arduino.

I would like to thank my parents to guide me to be a good human being.

www.PacktPub.com

Support files, eBooks, discount offers, and more

For support files and downloads related to your book, please visit www.PacktPub.com.

Did you know that Packt offers eBook versions of every book published, with PDF and ePub files available? You can upgrade to the eBook version at www.PacktPub. com and as a print book customer, you are entitled to a discount on the eBook copy. Get in touch with us at service@packtpub.com for more details.

At www.PacktPub.com, you can also read a collection of free technical articles, sign up for a range of free newsletters and receive exclusive discounts and offers on Packt books and eBooks.

https://www2.packtpub.com/books/subscription/packtlib

Do you need instant solutions to your IT questions? PacktLib is Packt's online digital book library. Here, you can search, access, and read Packt's entire library of books.

Why subscribe?

- Fully searchable across every book published by Packt
- Copy and paste, print, and bookmark content
- On demand and accessible via a web browser

Free access for Packt account holders

If you have an account with Packt at www.PacktPub.com, you can use this to access PacktLib today and view 9 entirely free books. Simply use your login credentials for immediate access.

Table of Contents

Table of Contents

Preface

An LED is a simple actuator device that displays lighting and can be controlled easily using Raspberry Pi. This book will explain processes to control LEDs using Raspberry Pi—from describing ideas to designing and implementing several projects based on LEDs, such as 7-segment, 4-digit 7-segment, and dot matrix displays. Samples of the project application are provided, such as a countdown timer, a digital clock, a traffic light controller, a remote light controller, and an LED-based Internet of Things, to get more practice with the Raspberry Pi development.

Raspberry Pi LED Blueprints is an essential reference for practical solutions to build the LED-based application. Beginning with step-by-step instructions for installation and configuration, this book can either be read from cover to cover or treated as an essential reference companion to your Raspberry Pi.

I hope that you will find this book useful and it will help you take your skills to a higher level.

What this book covers

Chapter 1, *Getting Started with LED Programming through Raspberry Pi GPIO*, helps you learn the basics of the Raspberry Pi GPIO and LED development so that you can be sure that you have the basics required to develop LED programming through Raspberry Pi GPIO.

Chapter 2, *Make Your Own Countdown Timer*, explains how to work with 7-segment displays and build a countdown timer. The basics of 7-segment display programming will be introduced. Furthermore, you will learn what shift register is and how to use it to enhance the handling of several 7-segment display modules.

Chapter 3, Make Your Own Digital Clock Display, explores how to build a digital clock. A digital clock is a type of clock that displays the time digitally using 4-digit 7-segment display modules. Furthermore, you will learn how to work with an OLED graphic display through an I2C interface and how to use it to build a digital clock.

Chapter 4, LED Dot Matrix, describes how to control an LED dot matrix with Raspberry Pi. At the end of the chapter, you will cascade several LED dot matrix modules and build a program to operate those modules.

Chapter 5, Building Your Own Traffic Light Controller, explains, in detail, how to build a traffic light controller using Raspberry Pi, from designing to implementing. Controlling AD/DC lamps using channel relay is introduced too.

Chapter 6, Building Your Own Light Controller-based Bluetooth, describes, in detail, how to build a light controller-based Bluetooth in a Raspberry Pi board. You can control the LEDs, lamps, or other devices from any device with a supporting Bluetooth stack, such as Android.

Chapter 7, Making Your Own Controlled Lamps through Internet Network, helps you make your own controlled lamps through the Internet network. You can control your LEDs, lamps, or other devices from any device with a supporting Internet network stack by utilizing RESTful. You will also learn how to build mobile application using PhoneGap and control LEDs from your mobile applications.

What you need for this book

You should have a Raspberry Pi board and several electronics components to run the projects in this book. You can configure and write programs to control LEDs using the Raspberry Pi board and mobile devices.

Who this book is for

This book is for those who want to learn how to build Raspberry Pi projects by utilizing LEDs, 7 segment, 4-digit 7-segment, and dot matrix modules. You will also learn to implement those modules in real applications, including interfacing with wireless modules and Android mobile apps. However, you don't need to have any previous experience with the Raspberry Pi or Android platforms.

Conventions

In this book, you will find a number of text styles that distinguish between different kinds of information. Here are some examples of these styles and an explanation of their meaning.

Code words in text, database table names, folder names, filenames, file extensions, pathnames, dummy URLs, user input, and Twitter handles are shown as follows: "Draw a rectangle using `canvas.rectangle()`."

A block of code is set as follows:

```
{
    "name": "chapter7",
    "version": "0.0.1",
    "dependencies":{
       "rpi-gpio": "latest",
       "async": "latest"
    }
}
```

Any command-line input or output is written as follows:

```
$ npm install rpi-gpio
```

New terms and **important words** are shown in bold. Words that you see on the screen, for example, in menus or dialog boxes, appear in the text like this: "If successful, you should see **spi_bcm2708** is loaded as shown."

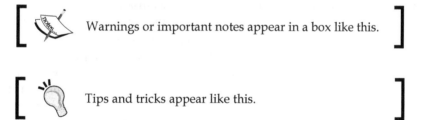

Warnings or important notes appear in a box like this.

Tips and tricks appear like this.

Reader feedback

Feedback from our readers is always welcome. Let us know what you think about this book—what you liked or disliked. Reader feedback is important for us as it helps us develop titles that you will really get the most out of.

To send us general feedback, simply e-mail `feedback@packtpub.com` and mention the book's title in the subject of your message.

If there is a topic that you have expertise in and you are interested in either writing or contributing to a book, see our author guide at `www.packtpub.com/authors`.

Customer support

Now that you are the proud owner of a Packt book, we have a number of things to help you to get the most from your purchase.

Downloading the example code

You can download the example code files from your account at `http://www.packtpub.com` for all the Packt Publishing books you have purchased. If you purchased this book elsewhere, you can visit `http://www.packtpub.com/support` and register to have the files e-mailed directly to you.

Errata

Although we have taken every care to ensure the accuracy of our content, mistakes do happen. If you find a mistake in one of our books—maybe a mistake in the text or the code—we would be grateful if you could report this to us. By doing so, you can save other readers from frustration and help us improve subsequent versions of this book. If you find any errata, please report them by visiting `http://www.packtpub.com/submit-errata`, selecting your book, clicking on the **Errata Submission Form** link, and entering the details of your errata. Once your errata are verified, your submission will be accepted and the errata will be uploaded to our website or added to any list of existing errata under the Errata section of that title.

To view the previously submitted errata, go to `https://www.packtpub.com/books/content/support` and enter the name of the book in the search field. The required information will appear under the **Errata** section.

Piracy

Piracy of copyrighted material on the Internet is an ongoing problem across all media. At Packt, we take the protection of our copyright and licenses very seriously. If you come across any illegal copies of our works in any form on the Internet, please provide us with the location address or website name immediately so that we can pursue a remedy.

Please contact us at copyright@packtpub.com with a link to the suspected pirated material.

We appreciate your help in protecting our authors and our ability to bring you valuable content.

Questions

If you have a problem with any aspect of this book, you can contact us at questions@packtpub.com, and we will do our best to address the problem.

1

Getting Started with LED Programming through Raspberry Pi GPIO

In this chapter, you will learn the basics of Raspberry Pi GPIO and LED development so that you can be sure that you have the basic required knowledge to develop LED programming through Raspberry Pi GPIO.

The following topics will be the major takeaways from this chapter:

- Setting up Raspberry Pi
- Introducing Raspberry Pi GPIO
- Blinking LEDs
- Turning an LED on/off using a push button
- Changing color through an RGB LED

Setting up Raspberry Pi

Raspberry Pi is a low-cost, credit card-sized computer that you can use to develop a general-purpose computer. There are several Raspberry Pi models that you can use to develop what you want. For illustration, this book will use a Raspberry Pi 2 board. Check `https://www.raspberrypi.org/products/`, which offers the Raspberry Pi 2 Model B board.

You can also see a video of the unboxing of Raspberry Pi 2 Model B from element14 on YouTube at `https://www.youtube.com/watch?v=1iavT62K5q8`.

To make Raspberry Pi work, we need an OS that acts as a *bridge* between the hardware and the user. There are many OS options that you can use for Raspberry Pi. This book uses Raspbian as an OS platform for Raspberry Pi. Raspbian OS is an operating system based on Debian with a targeting ARM processor. You can use another OS platform for Raspberry Pi from https://www.raspberrypi.org/downloads/. To deploy Raspbian with Raspberry Pi 2 Model B, we need a microSD card of at least 4 GB in size, but the recommended size is 8 GB. For testing purposes, we will use Raspbian as an operating system platform for Raspberry Pi.

You can set up your Raspberry Pi with the Raspbian image by following the instructions on this website, QUICK START GUIDE, https://www.raspberrypi.org/help/quick-start-guide/.

After having installed and deployed Raspbian, you can run the Raspbian desktop GUI by typing the following command on the terminal:

```
startx
```

This command makes Raspbian load the GUI module from the OS libraries. You can then see the Raspbian desktop GUI as follows:

Introducing Raspberry Pi GPIO

General-purpose input/output (GPIO) is a generic pin on Raspberry Pi, which can be used to interact with external devices, such as sensor and actuator devices. You can see the Raspberry Pi GPIO pinouts in the following figure (source: `http://www.element14.com/community/docs/DOC-73950/1/raspberry-pi-2-model-b-gpio-40-pin-block-pinout`):

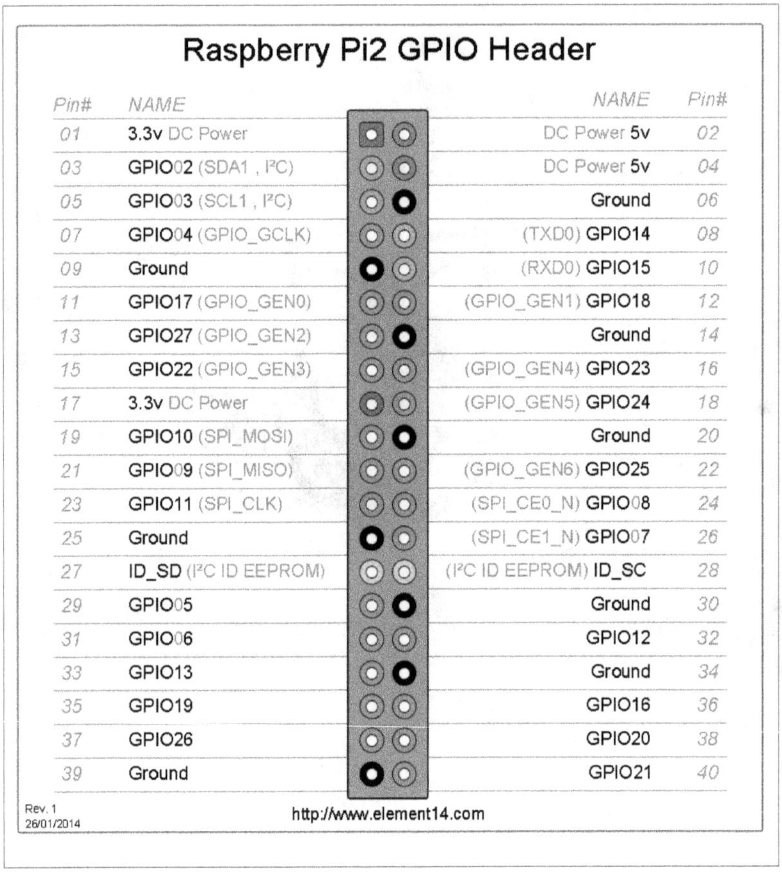

Raspberry Pi2 GPIO Header

Pin#	NAME			NAME	Pin#
01	3.3v DC Power	○	○	DC Power 5v	02
03	GPIO02 (SDA1 , I²C)	○	○	DC Power 5v	04
05	GPIO03 (SCL1 , I²C)	○	●	Ground	06
07	GPIO04 (GPIO_GCLK)	○	○	(TXD0) GPIO14	08
09	Ground	●	○	(RXD0) GPIO15	10
11	GPIO17 (GPIO_GEN0)	○	○	(GPIO_GEN1) GPIO18	12
13	GPIO27 (GPIO_GEN2)	○	●	Ground	14
15	GPIO22 (GPIO_GEN3)	○	○	(GPIO_GEN4) GPIO23	16
17	3.3v DC Power	○	○	(GPIO_GEN5) GPIO24	18
19	GPIO10 (SPI_MOSI)	●	○	Ground	20
21	GPIO09 (SPI_MISO)	○	○	(GPIO_GEN6) GPIO25	22
23	GPIO11 (SPI_CLK)	○	○	(SPI_CE0_N) GPIO08	24
25	Ground	●	○	(SPI_CE1_N) GPIO07	26
27	ID_SD (I²C ID EEPROM)	○	○	(I²C ID EEPROM) ID_SC	28
29	GPIO05	○	●	Ground	30
31	GPIO06	○	○	GPIO12	32
33	GPIO13	○	●	Ground	34
35	GPIO19	○	○	GPIO16	36
37	GPIO26	○	○	GPIO20	38
39	Ground	●	○	GPIO21	40

Rev. 1
26/01/2014

http://www.element14.com

To access Raspberry Pi GPIO, we can use several GPIO libraries. If you are working with Python, Raspbian will have already installed the `RPi.GPIO` library to access Raspberry Pi GPIO. You can read more about `RPi.GPIO` at `https://pypi.python.org/pypi/RPi.GPIO`. You can verify the `RPi.GPIO` library from a Python terminal by importing the `RPi.GPIO` module, as shown in the following screenshot:

```
pi@raspberrypi ~ $ python
Python 2.7.3 (default, Mar 18 2014, 05:13:23)
[GCC 4.6.3] on linux2
Type "help", "copyright", "credits" or "license" for more information.
>>> import RPi.GPIO as GPIO
>>> GPIO
<module 'RPi.GPIO' from '/usr/lib/python2.7/dist-packages/RPi/GPIO.so'>
>>>
```

If you don't find this library on Python runtime or get the error message
ImportError: No module named RPi.GPIO, you can install it by compiling from
the source code. For instance, we want to install RPi.GPIO 0.5.11, so type the
following commands:

```
wget hhttps://pypi.python.org/packages/source/R/RPi.GPIO/RPi.GPIO-0.5.11.
tar.gz
```

```
tar -xvzf RPi.GPIO-0.5.11.tar.gz
```

```
cd RPi.GPIO-0.5.11/
```

```
sudo python setup.py install
```

 To install and update through the apt command, your
Raspberry Pi must be connected to the Internet.

Another way to access Raspberry Pi GPIO is to use WiringPi. It is a library written
in C for Raspberry Pi to access GPIO pins. You can read information about WiringPi
from the official website http://wiringpi.com/.

To install WiringPi, you can type the following commands:

```
sudo apt-get update
```

```
sudo apt-get install git-core
```

```
git clone git://git.drogon.net/wiringPi
```

```
cd wiringPi
```

```
sudo ./build
```

Please make sure that your Pi network does not block the git protocol
for git://git.dragon.net/wiringPi. This code can be browsed on
https://git.drogon.net/?p=wiringPi;a=summary.

The next step is to install the WiringPi interface for Python, so you can access Raspberry Pi GPIO from a Python program. Type the following commands:

```
sudo apt-get install python-dev python-setuptools
git clone https://github.com/Gadgetoid/WiringPi2-Python.git
cd WiringPi2-Python
sudo python setup.py install
```

When finished, you can verify it by showing a GPIO map from the Raspberry Pi board using the GPIO tool:

```
gpio readall
```

If this is successful, you should see the GPIO map from the Raspberry Pi board on the terminal:

```
pi@raspberrypi ~ $ gpio readall
+-----+-----+---------+------+---+---Pi 2---+---+------+---------+-----+-----+
| BCM | wPi |   Name  | Mode | V | Physical | V | Mode |  Name   | wPi | BCM |
+-----+-----+---------+------+---+----++----+---+------+---------+-----+-----+
|     |     |    3.3v |      |   |  1 || 2  |   |      | 5v      |     |     |
|   2 |   8 |   SDA.1 |  IN  | 1 |  3 || 4  |   |      | 5V      |     |     |
|   3 |   9 |   SCL.1 |  IN  | 1 |  5 || 6  |   |      | 0v      |     |     |
|   4 |   7 | GPIO. 7 |  IN  | 1 |  7 || 8  | 1 | ALT0 | TxD     | 15  | 14  |
|     |     |      0v |      |   |  9 || 10 | 1 | ALT0 | RxD     | 16  | 15  |
|  17 |   0 | GPIO. 0 |  IN  | 0 | 11 || 12 | 0 | IN   | GPIO. 1 | 1   | 18  |
|  27 |   2 | GPIO. 2 |  IN  | 0 | 13 || 14 |   |      | 0v      |     |     |
|  22 |   3 | GPIO. 3 |  IN  | 0 | 15 || 16 | 0 | IN   | GPIO. 4 | 4   | 23  |
|     |     |    3.3v |      |   | 17 || 18 | 0 | IN   | GPIO. 5 | 5   | 24  |
|  10 |  12 |    MOSI |  IN  | 0 | 19 || 20 |   |      | 0v      |     |     |
|   9 |  13 |    MISO |  IN  | 0 | 21 || 22 | 0 | IN   | GPIO. 6 | 6   | 25  |
|  11 |  14 |    SCLK |  IN  | 0 | 23 || 24 | 1 | IN   | CE0     | 10  | 8   |
|     |     |      0v |      |   | 25 || 26 | 1 | IN   | CE1     | 11  | 7   |
|   0 |  30 |   SDA.0 |  IN  | 1 | 27 || 28 | 1 | IN   | SCL.0   | 31  | 1   |
|   5 |  21 | GPIO.21 |  IN  | 1 | 29 || 30 |   |      | 0v      |     |     |
|   6 |  22 | GPIO.22 |  IN  | 1 | 31 || 32 | 0 | IN   | GPIO.26 | 26  | 12  |
|  13 |  23 | GPIO.23 |  IN  | 0 | 33 || 34 |   |      | 0v      |     |     |
|  19 |  24 | GPIO.24 |  IN  | 0 | 35 || 36 | 0 | IN   | GPIO.27 | 27  | 16  |
|  26 |  25 | GPIO.25 |  IN  | 0 | 37 || 38 | 0 | IN   | GPIO.28 | 28  | 20  |
|     |     |      0v |      |   | 39 || 40 | 0 | IN   | GPIO.29 | 29  | 21  |
+-----+-----+---------+------+---+----++----+---+------+---------+-----+-----+
| BCM | wPi |   Name  | Mode | V | Physical | V | Mode |  Name   | wPi | BCM |
+-----+-----+---------+------+---+---Pi 2---+---+------+---------+-----+-----+
pi@raspberrypi ~ $
```

You can also see values in the **wPi** column, which will be used in the WiringPi program as GPIO value parameters. I will show you how to use it in the WiringPi library in the next section.

Blinking LEDs

In this section, we will build a simple app that interacts with Raspberry Pi GPIO. We will use three LEDs, which are attached to the Raspberry Pi 2 board. Furthermore, we will turn the LEDs on/off sequentially.

The following hardware components are needed:

- Raspberry Pi 2.(you can change this model)
- Three LEDs of any color
- Three resistors (330 Ω or 220 Ω)

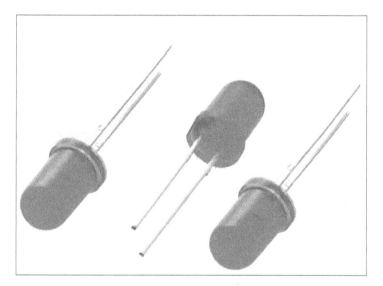

The hardware wiring can be implemented as follows:

- LED 1 is connected to Pi *GPIO18*
- LED 2 is connected to Pi *GPIO23*
- LED 3 is connected to Pi *GPIO24*

The following image shows the hardware connection for LED blinking:

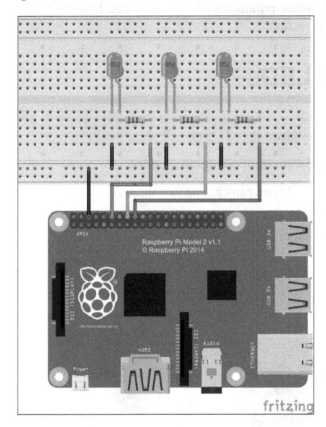

Now you can write a program using WiringPi with Python. The following is the complete Python code for blinking LEDs:

```python
# ch01_01.py file

import wiringpi2 as wiringpi
import time

# initialize
wiringpi.wiringPiSetup()

# define GPIO mode
GPIO18 = 1
GPIO23 = 4
GPIO24 = 5
```

```
LOW = 0
HIGH = 1
OUTPUT = 1
wiringpi.pinMode(GPIO18, OUTPUT)
wiringpi.pinMode(GPIO23, OUTPUT)
wiringpi.pinMode(GPIO24, OUTPUT)


# make all LEDs off
def clear_all():
    wiringpi.digitalWrite(GPIO18, LOW)
    wiringpi.digitalWrite(GPIO23, LOW)
    wiringpi.digitalWrite(GPIO24, LOW)

# turn on LED sequentially
try:
    while 1:
        clear_all()
        print("turn on LED 1")
        wiringpi.digitalWrite(GPIO18, HIGH)
        time.sleep(2)
        clear_all()
        print("turn on LED 2")
        wiringpi.digitalWrite(GPIO23, HIGH)
        time.sleep(2)
        clear_all()
        print("turn on LED 3")
        wiringpi.digitalWrite(GPIO24, HIGH)
        time.sleep(2)

except KeyboardInterrupt:
    clear_all()

print("done")
```

Save this script in a file named Python ch01_01.py.

Moreover, you can run this file on the terminal. Type the following command:

```
sudo python ch01_01.py
```

You should see three LEDs blinking sequentially. To stop the program, you can press *CTRL+C* on the Pi terminal. The following is a sample of the program output:

```
pi@raspberrypi: ~/led
pi@raspberrypi ~/led $ sudo python ch01_01.py
turn on LED 1
turn on LED 2
turn on LED 3
turn on LED 1
turn on LED 2
turn on LED 3
turn on LED 1
^Cdone
pi@raspberrypi ~/led $
```

Based on our wiring, we connect three LEDs to *GPIO18*, *GPIO23*, and *GPIO24* from the Raspberry Pi board. You can see these WiringPi GPIO values from the `gpio readall` command and find *GPIO18*, *GPIO23*, and *GPIO24* recognized as (the **wPi** column) 1, 4, and 5, respectively.

First, we initialize WiringPi using `wiringpi.wiringPiSetup()`. Then, we define our GPIO values and set their modes on Raspberry Pi as follows:

```
GPIO18 = 1
GPIO23 = 4
GPIO24 = 5
LOW = 0
HIGH = 1
OUTPUT = 1
wiringpi.pinMode(GPIO18, OUTPUT)
wiringpi.pinMode(GPIO23, OUTPUT)
wiringpi.pinMode(GPIO24, OUTPUT)
```

Each LED will be turned on using `wiringpi.digitalWrite()`. `time.sleep(n)` is used to hold the program for *n* seconds. Let's set a delay time of two seconds as follows:

```
clear_all()
print("turn on LED 1")
wiringpi.digitalWrite(GPIO18, HIGH)
time.sleep(2)
```

The `clear_all()` function is designed to turn off all LEDs:

```
def clear_all():
    wiringpi.digitalWrite(GPIO18, LOW)
    wiringpi.digitalWrite(GPIO23, LOW)
    wiringpi.digitalWrite(GPIO24, LOW)
```

Turning an LED on/off using a push button

In the previous section, we accessed Raspberry Pi GPIO to turn LEDs on/off by program. Now we will learn how to turn an LED on/off using a push button, which is used as a GPIO input from Raspberry Pi GPIO.

The following hardware components are needed:

- A Raspberry Pi 2 board
- An LED
- A push button (`https://www.sparkfun.com/products/97`)
- 1 KΩ resistor

You can see the push button connection in the following figure:

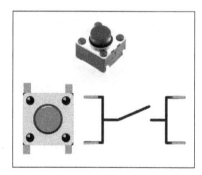

Our hardware wiring is simple. You simply connect the LED to *GPIO23* from Raspberry Pi. The push button is connected to Raspberry Pi GPIO on *GPIO24*. The complete hardware wiring can be seen in the following figure:

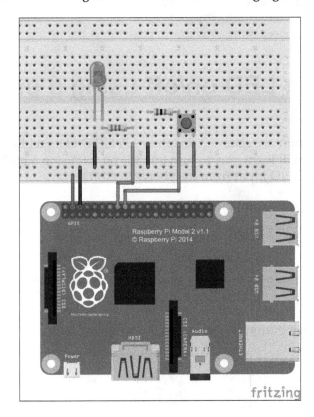

Furthermore, you can write a Python program to read the push button's state. If you press the push button, the program will turn on the LED. Otherwise, it will turn off the LED. This is our program scenario.

The following is the complete code for the Python program:

```
# ch01_02.py file

import wiringpi2 as wiringpi

# initialize
wiringpi.wiringPiSetup()

# define GPIO mode
GPIO23 = 4
GPIO24 = 5
LOW = 0
```

```
HIGH = 1
OUTPUT = 1
INPUT = 0
PULL_DOWN = 1
wiringpi.pinMode(GPIO23, OUTPUT)   # LED
wiringpi.pinMode(GPIO24, INPUT)    # push button
wiringpi.pullUpDnControl(GPIO24, PULL_DOWN)   # pull down


# make all LEDs off
def clear_all():
    wiringpi.digitalWrite(GPIO23, LOW)

try:
    clear_all()
    while 1:
        button_state = wiringpi.digitalRead(GPIO24)
        print button_state
        if button_state == 1:
            wiringpi.digitalWrite(GPIO23, HIGH)
        else:
            wiringpi.digitalWrite(GPIO23, LOW)

        wiringpi.delay(20)

except KeyboardInterrupt:
    clear_all()

print("done")
```

Save this code in a file named ch01_02.py.

Now you can run this program via the terminal:

```
$ sudo python ch01_02.py
```

After this, you can check by pressing the push button; you should see the LED lighting up.

First, we define our Raspberry Pi GPIO's usage. We also declare our GPIO input to be set as pull down. This means that if the push button is pressed, it will return value *1*.

```
GPIO23 = 4
GPIO24 = 5
LOW = 0
HIGH = 1
OUTPUT = 1
INPUT = 0
PULL_DOWN = 1
```

```
wiringpi.pinMode(GPIO23, OUTPUT)   # LED
wiringpi.pinMode(GPIO24, INPUT)    # push button
wiringpi.pullUpDnControl(GPIO24, PULL_DOWN)   # pull down
```

We can read the push button's state using the `digitalRead()` function from WiringPi as follows:

```
button_state = wiringpi.digitalRead(GPIO24)
```

If the push button is pressed, we turn on the LED; otherwise, we turn it off:

```
print button_state
if button_state == 1:
    wiringpi.digitalWrite(GPIO23, HIGH)
else:
    wiringpi.digitalWrite(GPIO23, LOW)
```

Changing color through an RGB LED

The last demo of basic LED programming is to work with an RGB LED. This LED can emit monochromatic light, which could be one of the three primary colors — **red, green, and blue**, known as **RGB**.

The RGB LED connection is shown in the following figure:

In this section, we will build a simple program to display red, green, and blue colors through the RGB LED.

The following hardware components are needed:

- A Raspberry Pi 2 board
- An RGB LED (`https://www.sparkfun.com/products/9264`).

Our hardware wiring can be implemented as follows:

- RGB LED pin *1* is connected to Raspberry Pi *GPIO18*
- RGB LED pin *2* is connected to Raspberry Pi *VCC +3 V*
- RGB LED pin *3* is connected to Raspberry Pi *GPIO23*
- RGB LED pin *4* is connected to Raspberry Pi *GPIO24*

The complete hardware wiring can be seen in the following figure:

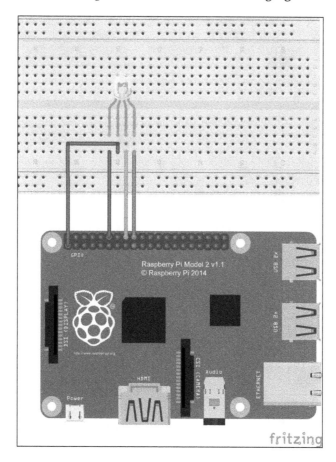

Returning to the Raspberry Pi terminal, you could write a Python program to display color through RGB LED. Let's create a file named `ch01_03.py` and write this script as follows:

```python
# ch01_03.py file

import wiringpi2 as wiringpi
import time

# initialize
wiringpi.wiringPiSetup()

# define GPIO mode
GPIO18 = 1  # red
GPIO23 = 4  # green
GPIO24 = 5  # blue
LOW = 0
HIGH = 1
OUTPUT = 1
wiringpi.pinMode(GPIO18, OUTPUT)
wiringpi.pinMode(GPIO23, OUTPUT)
wiringpi.pinMode(GPIO24, OUTPUT)


# make all LEDs off
def clear_all():
    wiringpi.digitalWrite(GPIO18, HIGH)
    wiringpi.digitalWrite(GPIO23, HIGH)
    wiringpi.digitalWrite(GPIO24, HIGH)


def display(red, green, blue):
    wiringpi.digitalWrite(GPIO18, red)
    wiringpi.digitalWrite(GPIO23, green)
    wiringpi.digitalWrite(GPIO24, blue)


try:
    while 1:
        clear_all()
```

```
        print("red")
        display(0, 1, 1)
        time.sleep(2)
        clear_all()
        print("green")
        display(1, 0, 1)
        time.sleep(2)
        clear_all()
        print("blue")
        display(1, 1, 0)
        time.sleep(2)
        clear_all()
        print("white")
        display(0, 0, 0)
        time.sleep(2)
        clear_all()
        print("110")
        display(1, 1, 0)
        time.sleep(2)
        clear_all()
        print("101")
        display(1, 0, 1)
        time.sleep(2)
        clear_all()
        print("011")
        display(0, 1, 1)
        time.sleep(2)

except KeyboardInterrupt:
    clear_all()

print("done")
```

Save this script. You can run this file by typing the following command:

```
$ sudo python ch01_03.py
```

Then, you should see that the RGB LED displays a certain color every second. The program output can also write a message indicating which color is currently on the RGB LED:

```
                                              pi@raspberrypi: ~/led
pi@raspberrypi ~/led $ sudo python ch01_03.py
red
green
blue
white
110
101
011
red
green
blue
white
110
101
011
red
green
blue
```

The RGB LED can display a color by combining three basic colors: red, green, and blue. First, we initialize Raspberry Pi GPIO and define our GPIO usage:

```
# initialize
wiringpi.wiringPiSetup()

# define GPIO mode
GPIO18 = 1  # red
GPIO23 = 4  # green
GPIO24 = 5  # blue
LOW = 0
HIGH = 1
OUTPUT = 1
wiringpi.pinMode(GPIO18, OUTPUT)
wiringpi.pinMode(GPIO23, OUTPUT)
wiringpi.pinMode(GPIO24, OUTPUT)
```

For instance, to set a red color, we should set LOW on the red pin and HIGH on both green and blue pins. We define the display() function to display a certain color on the RGB LED with the red, green, and blue values as parameters as follows:

```
def display(red, green, blue):
    wiringpi.digitalWrite(GPIO18, red)
    wiringpi.digitalWrite(GPIO23, green)
    wiringpi.digitalWrite(GPIO24, blue)
```

In the main program, we display a color via the display() function by passing red, green, and blue values, as shown in the following code:

```
clear_all()
print("red")
display(0, 1, 1)
time.sleep(2)
clear_all()
print("green")
display(1, 0, 1)
time.sleep(2)
clear_all()
print("blue")
display(1, 1, 0)
time.sleep(2)
clear_all()
print("white")
display(0, 0, 0)
time.sleep(2)
clear_all()
print("110")
display(1, 1, 0)
time.sleep(2)
clear_all()
print("101")
display(1, 0, 1)
time.sleep(2)
clear_all()
print("011")
display(0, 1, 1)
time.sleep(2)
```

Summary

Let's summarize what we have learned in this chapter. We connected three LEDs to a Raspberry Pi board. After that, we made these LEDs blink. Then, we read the Raspberry Pi GPIO input. Finally, we learned to display several colors through an RGB LED.

In the next chapter, we will work with 7-segment display and a shift register to manipulate several 7-segment display modules. We will also build a countdown timer app by utilizing a 7-segment module.

2

Make Your Own
Countdown Timer

In this chapter, we will learn how to work with a 7-segment display. Then we will build a countdown timer. The basics of 7-segment display programming will be introduced. Furthermore, we will learn what a shift register is and how to use it to enhance the handling of several 7-segment display modules.

From this chapter, you will learn the following topics:

- Introducing a 7-segment display
- Introducing a shift register
- Driving a 7-segment display using a shift register
- Working with the 4-digit 7-segment display
- Building a countdown timer

Introducing a 7-segment display

In general, a 7-segment display consists of seven LEDs, and an additional LED is used for a dot (DP pin). This then allows us to display each of the 10 decimal digits 0 to 9 on the same 7-segment display.

There are two types of LED 7-segment displays, named **common cathode (CC)** and **common anode (CA)**. Each LED has two connecting pins: the **anode** and the **cathode**. A sample LED datasheet can be found at `http://www.kitronik.co.uk/pdf/7_segment_display_datasheet.pdf`.

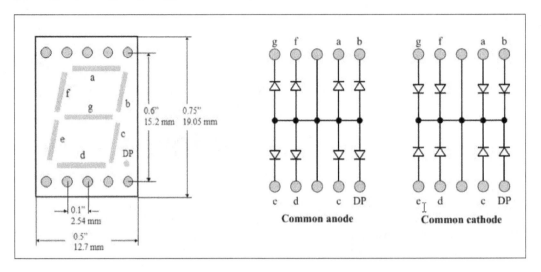

We can show a number on the 7-segment display by combining LED lighting through its pins. For instance, if we want to display the number 7, we should turn on LEDs *a*, *b*, and *c*. To turn an LED on/off, we can use Raspberry Pi GPIO:

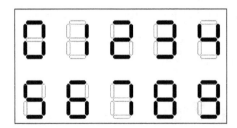

Furthermore, we are going to build a program to display the numbers 0 to 9 using Python. The following is the hardware required:

- A Raspberry Pi 2 board
- A 7-segment display of the CC model (red, `https://www.sparkfun.com/products/8546`, or blue, `https://www.sparkfun.com/products/9191`)
- A breadboard (refer to `https://www.sparkfun.com/products/12002`)
- Cables

The hardware wiring can be implemented as follows:

- 7-segment display pin *a* — Raspberry Pi *GPIO14*
- 7-segment display pin *b* — Raspberry Pi *GPIO15*
- 7-segment display pin *c* — Raspberry Pi *GPIO18*
- 7-segment display pin *DP* — Raspberry Pi *GPIO23*
- 7-segment display pin *d* — Raspberry Pi *GPIO24*
- 7-segment display pin *e* — Raspberry Pi *GPIO25*
- 7-segment display pin *f* — Raspberry Pi *GPIO8*
- 7-segment display pin *g* — Raspberry Pi *GPIO7*
- 7-segment display common pin (common anode) — Raspberry Pi *GND*

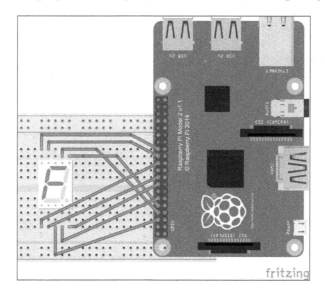

Now we know the hardware wiring, we can write a program to display a number on the 7-segment display using Python. Create a file named ch02_01.py. The following is the complete code for the ch02_01.py file:

```
# ch02_01.py file

import wiringpi2 as wiringpi
import time

# initialize
wiringpi.wiringPiSetup()
```

```
# define GPIO pins
pin_a = 15
pin_b = 16
pin_c = 1
pin_dip = 4
pin_d = 5
pin_e = 6
pin_f = 10
pin_g = 11

LOW = 0
HIGH = 1
OUTPUT = 1
# define GPIO mode
wiringpi.pinMode(pin_a, OUTPUT)
wiringpi.pinMode(pin_b, OUTPUT)
wiringpi.pinMode(pin_c, OUTPUT)
wiringpi.pinMode(pin_dip, OUTPUT)
wiringpi.pinMode(pin_d, OUTPUT)
wiringpi.pinMode(pin_e, OUTPUT)
wiringpi.pinMode(pin_f, OUTPUT)
wiringpi.pinMode(pin_g, OUTPUT)


def showNumber(number, dip):
    if dip:
        wiringpi.digitalWrite(pin_dip, HIGH)
    else:
        wiringpi.digitalWrite(pin_dip, LOW)

    if number == 0:
        wiringpi.digitalWrite(pin_a, HIGH)
        wiringpi.digitalWrite(pin_b, HIGH)
        wiringpi.digitalWrite(pin_c, HIGH)
        wiringpi.digitalWrite(pin_d, HIGH)
        wiringpi.digitalWrite(pin_e, HIGH)
        wiringpi.digitalWrite(pin_f, HIGH)
        wiringpi.digitalWrite(pin_g, LOW)
    elif number == 1:
        wiringpi.digitalWrite(pin_a, LOW)
        wiringpi.digitalWrite(pin_b, HIGH)
        wiringpi.digitalWrite(pin_c, HIGH)
        wiringpi.digitalWrite(pin_d, LOW)
        wiringpi.digitalWrite(pin_e, LOW)
```

```
        wiringpi.digitalWrite(pin_f, LOW)
        wiringpi.digitalWrite(pin_g, LOW)
    elif number == 2:
        wiringpi.digitalWrite(pin_a, HIGH)
        wiringpi.digitalWrite(pin_b, HIGH)
        wiringpi.digitalWrite(pin_c, LOW)
        wiringpi.digitalWrite(pin_d, HIGH)
        wiringpi.digitalWrite(pin_e, HIGH)
        wiringpi.digitalWrite(pin_f, LOW)
        wiringpi.digitalWrite(pin_g, HIGH)
    elif number == 3:
        wiringpi.digitalWrite(pin_a, HIGH)
        wiringpi.digitalWrite(pin_b, HIGH)
        wiringpi.digitalWrite(pin_c, HIGH)
        wiringpi.digitalWrite(pin_d, HIGH)
        wiringpi.digitalWrite(pin_e, LOW)
        wiringpi.digitalWrite(pin_f, LOW)
        wiringpi.digitalWrite(pin_g, HIGH)
    elif number == 4:
        wiringpi.digitalWrite(pin_a, LOW)
        wiringpi.digitalWrite(pin_b, HIGH)
        wiringpi.digitalWrite(pin_c, HIGH)
        wiringpi.digitalWrite(pin_d, LOW)
        wiringpi.digitalWrite(pin_e, LOW)
        wiringpi.digitalWrite(pin_f, HIGH)
        wiringpi.digitalWrite(pin_g, HIGH)
    elif number == 5:
        wiringpi.digitalWrite(pin_a, HIGH)
        wiringpi.digitalWrite(pin_b, LOW)
        wiringpi.digitalWrite(pin_c, HIGH)
        wiringpi.digitalWrite(pin_d, HIGH)
        wiringpi.digitalWrite(pin_e, LOW)
        wiringpi.digitalWrite(pin_f, HIGH)
        wiringpi.digitalWrite(pin_g, HIGH)
    elif number == 6:
        wiringpi.digitalWrite(pin_a, HIGH)
        wiringpi.digitalWrite(pin_b, LOW)
        wiringpi.digitalWrite(pin_c, HIGH)
        wiringpi.digitalWrite(pin_d, HIGH)
        wiringpi.digitalWrite(pin_e, HIGH)
        wiringpi.digitalWrite(pin_f, HIGH)
        wiringpi.digitalWrite(pin_g, HIGH)
    elif number == 7:
        wiringpi.digitalWrite(pin_a, HIGH)
```

```
            wiringpi.digitalWrite(pin_b, HIGH)
            wiringpi.digitalWrite(pin_c, HIGH)
            wiringpi.digitalWrite(pin_d, LOW)
            wiringpi.digitalWrite(pin_e, LOW)
            wiringpi.digitalWrite(pin_f, LOW)
            wiringpi.digitalWrite(pin_g, LOW)
        elif number == 8:
            wiringpi.digitalWrite(pin_a, HIGH)
            wiringpi.digitalWrite(pin_b, HIGH)
            wiringpi.digitalWrite(pin_c, HIGH)
            wiringpi.digitalWrite(pin_d, HIGH)
            wiringpi.digitalWrite(pin_e, HIGH)
            wiringpi.digitalWrite(pin_f, HIGH)
            wiringpi.digitalWrite(pin_g, HIGH)
        elif number == 9:
            wiringpi.digitalWrite(pin_a, HIGH)
            wiringpi.digitalWrite(pin_b, HIGH)
            wiringpi.digitalWrite(pin_c, HIGH)
            wiringpi.digitalWrite(pin_d, HIGH)
            wiringpi.digitalWrite(pin_e, LOW)
            wiringpi.digitalWrite(pin_f, HIGH)
            wiringpi.digitalWrite(pin_g, HIGH)


def clear_all():
    wiringpi.digitalWrite(pin_a, LOW)
    wiringpi.digitalWrite(pin_b, LOW)
    wiringpi.digitalWrite(pin_c, LOW)
    wiringpi.digitalWrite(pin_d, LOW)
    wiringpi.digitalWrite(pin_e, LOW)
    wiringpi.digitalWrite(pin_f, LOW)
    wiringpi.digitalWrite(pin_g, LOW)
    wiringpi.digitalWrite(pin_dip, LOW)

try:
    while 1:
        print("display 0")
        showNumber(0, HIGH)
        time.sleep(2)

        print("display 1")
        showNumber(1, HIGH)
```

```
            time.sleep(2)

            print("display 2")
            showNumber(2, HIGH)
            time.sleep(2)

            print("display 3")
            showNumber(3, HIGH)
            time.sleep(2)

            print("display 4")
            showNumber(4, HIGH)
            time.sleep(2)

            print("display 5")
            showNumber(5, HIGH)
            time.sleep(2)

            print("display 6")
            showNumber(6, HIGH)
            time.sleep(2)

            print("display 7")
            showNumber(7, HIGH)
            time.sleep(2)

            print("display 8")
            showNumber(8, HIGH)
            time.sleep(2)

            print("display 9")
            showNumber(9, HIGH)
            time.sleep(2)

            clear_all()

    except KeyboardInterrupt:
        clear_all()

    print("done")
```

This code can be explained as follows:

- First, we define the Raspberry Pi GPIO and set them as the output mode

- The DP pin from the 7-segment display is declared as a `dip` variable. It's used to display a dot on the 7-segment display. If you set it `HIGH`, the dot on the 7-segment display will be visible

- Declare the `showNumber()` function to show a number on the 7-segment display by combining lighting LEDs by passing the `HIGH` value to Raspberry Pi GPIO. It uses the `digitalWrite()` function from the WiringPi library. The `showNumber()` function also needs a `dip` value. If you pass the `HIGH` value, the 7-segment module will show a dot, which is located at the bottom-right. If you set it `LOW`, the 7-segment dot will not be shown.

- Declare `clear_all()` to turn off all LEDs on the 7-segment display. This is done by passing a `LOW` value on all GPIO pins

- The program does a looping and displays a number from 0 to 9 by calling the `showNumber()` function and passing `dip` with `HIGH` to show the 7-segment's dot

To run this program, you can type the following command on a terminal.

```
sudo python ch02_01.py
```

If this is successful, the 7-segment display shows a number from 0 to 9. You also see a message on the terminal as follows:

```
pi@raspberrypi ~/led $ sudo python ch02_01.py
display 0
display 1
display 2
display 3
display 4
display 5
display 6
display 7
display 8
display 9
display 0
display 1
display 2
```

Introducing a shift register

If our project needs to control 32 LEDs, we would normally require 32 pins of a **microcontroller (MCU)**. The problem is that every MCU has a limited number of pins for GPIO. To address this issue, we can extend our MCU GPIO pins.

One of the solutions to extend GPIO pins is to use a shift register. We can use 74HC595 to extend the GPIO output pins. If you want to extend the GPIO input pins, you can use 74HC165. The schema of 74HC595 can be seen in the following figure:

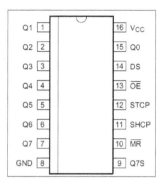

The *Q0* to *Q7* pins are the parallel output from the chip. The *DS* pin is the serial data. *STCP* is the latch pin, and *SHCP* is the clock pin.

In this section, you will see how to implement a shift register to extend Raspberry Pi GPIO output pins using IC 74HC595 (Sparkfun, https://www.sparkfun.com/products/733). We need eight LEDs for the demonstration. The program will turn on only one LED at a time. It starts from LED 1 to 8. The hardware wiring is shown in the following figure:

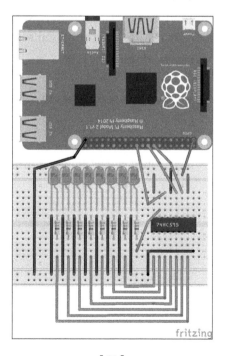

When the output enable (*OE*) input is high, the outputs are in the high-impedance state. Otherwise, (*OE*) input is high. Data in the storage register appears at the output whenever the output enable input (*OE*) is low. A low level on **Master reset** (**MR**) only affects the shift registers. So in this scenario, we set +3.3 V on the *MR* pin.

The hardware wiring is as follows:

- 74HC595 *Q0* to *Q7* pins are connected to the LEDs
- The 74HC595 *VCC* pin is connected to Raspberry Pi *VCC* (+3.3 V)
- The 74HC595 *GND* pin is connected to Raspberry Pi *GND*
- The 74HC595 *DS/Data* pin is connected to Raspberry Pi *GPIO25* (wPi 6)
- The 74HC595 *OE* pin is connected to Raspberry Pi GPIO *GND*
- The 74HC595 *STCP/LATCH* pin is connected to Raspberry Pi *GPIO24* (wPi 5)
- The 74HC595 *SHCP/Clock* pin is connected to Raspberry Pi *GPIO23* (wPi 4)
- The 74HC595 *MR* pin is connected to Raspberry Pi GPIO *VCC* +3.3 V

To write data into 74HC595, we perform the following steps based on the timing diagram, as shown in the following figure, from the IC's datasheet (`http://www.nxp.com/documents/data_sheet/74HC_HCT595.pdf`). In the program implementation, we perform the following steps:

1. Set your data value on the *DS/Data* pin. It could be high or low.
2. Send a pulse (high to low) to the *Clock* pin. To implement a pulse, you can set the high value on the *SHCP/Clock* pin and then set the low value.
3. If you work with 8-bit serial data, then follow steps 1 and 2 for each bit for your 8-bit data.
4. When finished, you can store this serial data by sending a pulse (high to low) to the *STCP/LATCH* pin.

74HC595 can receive 8-bit serial data. So if you have more than 8-bit serial data, follow steps 1 to 4 for each 8-bit serial data.

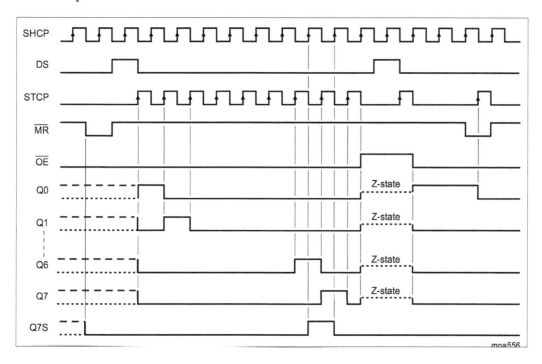

The next step is to write a program to implement the shift register using Python with the WiringPi library. The code is ported from http://www.bristolwatch.com/ele2/74HC595_cylon.htm, so it can work with WiringPi for Python:

Create a file named ch02_02.py and write the following complete code:

```
# ch02_02.py file

import wiringpi2 as wiringpi
import time

# initialize
wiringpi.wiringPiSetup()   # WiPi mode

# define shift reg pins
DATA = 6
```

```python
LATCH = 5
CLK = 4

OUTPUT = 1
LOW = 0
HIGH = 1

wiringpi.pinMode(DATA, OUTPUT)
wiringpi.pinMode(LATCH, OUTPUT)
wiringpi.pinMode(CLK, OUTPUT)

# initialization
print("Initialization...")
wiringpi.digitalWrite(LATCH, LOW)
wiringpi.digitalWrite(CLK, LOW)


def pulse_clock():
    wiringpi.digitalWrite(CLK, HIGH)
    wiringpi.digitalWrite(CLK, LOW)
    return


def serial_latch():
    wiringpi.digitalWrite(LATCH, HIGH)
    wiringpi.digitalWrite(LATCH, LOW)
    return


def ssr_write(value):
    for i in range(0, 8):
        val = value & 0x80
        if val == 0x80:
            wiringpi.digitalWrite(DATA, HIGH)
        else:
            wiringpi.digitalWrite(DATA, LOW)

        pulse_clock()
        value <<= 0x01  # shift left
    serial_latch()
    return


try:
```

```
    while 1:
        digit = 1
        for i in range(0, 8):
            print(digit)
            ssr_write(digit)
            digit <<= 1
            time.sleep(0.5)

        for i in range(0, 8):
            digit >>= 1
            print(digit)
            ssr_write(digit)
            time.sleep(0.5)

except KeyboardInterrupt:
    ssr_write(0)

print("done")
```

Here is the code explanation:

- The program starts by defining DATA, LATCH, and CLK pins. It uses the WiPi pin mode. You may change it using the GPIO BCM mode.
- Set DATA, LATCH, and CLK pins as the output mode.
- Initialize IC 74HC595 by sending the LOW value to the LATCH and CLK pins.
- Declare the pulse_clock() and serial_latch() functions.
- To write data into IC 74HC595, we declare the ssr_write() function.
- In the main program, the ssr_write() function writes data 1 and then shifts the data left and right.

Shifting bits uses bitwise operators. << is left shifting and >> is right shifting. Please refer to https://wiki.python.org/moin/BitwiseOperators and https://wiki.python.org/moin/BitManipulation. For example, you have data on x = 0b00000001. x <<= 1 gets output x = 0b00000010. If you have x = 0b00000010 and if you set x >>= 1, you will get x = 0b00000001.

Now you can run this program by typing the following command on the terminal:

```
sudo python ch02_02.py
```

If it is successful, you should see that the lighting works from LED 1 to LED 8. Then, it turns back. You can see this demonstration in my YouTube, https://youtu.be/UDPBVbjU63s.

Driving a 7-segment display using a shift register

We have already learned how to use a shift register using 74HC595. In this section, we will try to use a shift register to drive a 7-segment display.

To drive a 7-segment display using a shift register, you can connect 74HC595 to the 7-segment module. The following is the hardware wiring:

- 74HC595 *Q0* to *Q6* pins to 7-segment *a* to *b* pins
- The 74HC595 *Q7* pin to the 7-segment *DP* pin
- The 74HC595 *VCC* pin is connected to Raspberry Pi *VCC* +3.3 V
- The 74HC595 *GND* pin is connected to Raspberry Pi *GND*
- The 74HC595 *DS/Data* pin is connected to Raspberry Pi *GPIO25* (wPi 6)
- The 74HC595 *OE* pin is connected to Raspberry Pi GPIO *GND*
- The 74HC595 *STCP/LATCH* pin is connected to Raspberry Pi *GPIO24* (wPi 5)
- The 74HC595 *SHCP/Clock* pin is connected to Raspberry Pi *GPIO23* (wPi 4)
- The 74HC595 *MR* pin is connected to Raspberry Pi GPIO *VCC* +3.3 V

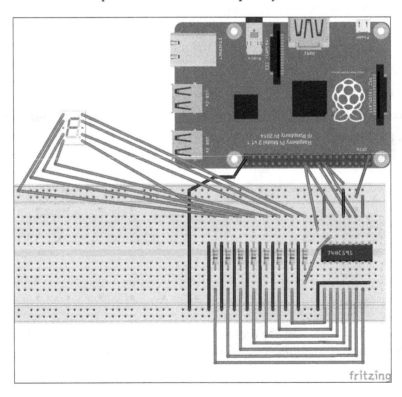

You can see that there are resistors on the wiring. These components are used to prevent the higher current flow on you wiring so a resistor keeps your IC module safe. You can ignore these components if you can guarantee the safe current flow on the circuit.

The next step is to write a program. In this scenario, we are going to display the numbers from 0 to 9. Create a file, named ch02_03.py, and write the following complete code:

```
# ch02_03.py file

import wiringpi2 as wiringpi
import time

# initialize
wiringpi.wiringPiSetup()  # WiPi mode

# define shift reg pins
DATA = 6
LATCH = 5
CLK = 4

OUTPUT = 1
LOW = 0
HIGH = 1

# segment 0, 1, 2, 3, 4, 5, 6, 7, 8, 9
# format: hgfedcba
## for 7-segment common cathode. For common anode, change 1 to 0, 0 to
1.
segments = [0b00111111, 0b00000110, 0b01011011, 0b01001111,
            0b01100110, 0b01101101, 0b01111101, 0b00000111,
0b01111111, 0b01101111]


wiringpi.pinMode(DATA, OUTPUT)
wiringpi.pinMode(LATCH, OUTPUT)
wiringpi.pinMode(CLK, OUTPUT)

# initialization
print("Initialization...")
wiringpi.digitalWrite(LATCH, LOW)
```

```python
        wiringpi.digitalWrite(CLK, LOW)


def pulse_clock():
    wiringpi.digitalWrite(CLK, HIGH)
    wiringpi.digitalWrite(CLK, LOW)
    return


def serial_latch():
    wiringpi.digitalWrite(LATCH, HIGH)
    wiringpi.digitalWrite(LATCH, LOW)
    return


def ssr_write(value):
    for i in range(0, 8):
        val = value & 0x80
        if val == 0x80:
            wiringpi.digitalWrite(DATA, HIGH)
        else:
            wiringpi.digitalWrite(DATA, LOW)

        pulse_clock()
        value <<= 0x01   # shift left
    serial_latch()
    return


try:
    digit = 0
    while 1:
        print(digit)
        ssr_write(segments[digit])
        time.sleep(0.5)
        digit += 1
        if digit > 9:
            digit = 0
```

```
except KeyboardInterrupt:
    ssr_write(0)

print("done")
```

Basically, this program is the result of modified code from ch02_02.py. In this scenario, we connect 74HC595 segment output pins to the 7-segment display. Then, we construct a collection of numbers by combining lighting LEDs. The format is *hgfedcba*.

```
segments = [0b00111111, 0b00000110, 0b01011011, 0b01001111,
            0b01100110, 0b01101101, 0b01111101, 0b00000111,
            0b01111111, 0b01101111]
```

The ssr_write() function is used to display data on the 7-segment display by passing a value parameter. Value is byte data. To send one byte (8-bit data), we do a looping and get one bit starting from the left. To implement this, we can use the left shifting:

```
value <<= 0x01
```

The program will display the numbers from 0 to 9 by passing a value from a collection of numbers:

```
digit = 0
while 1:
    print(digit)
    ssr_write(segments[digit])
    time.sleep(0.5)
    digit += 1
    if digit > 9:
        digit = 0
```

Save this file. Now you can run this program.

```
sudo python ch02_03.py
```

If it gets success, you should see a number on the 7-segment display module. You can see this demo in my YouTube, http://youtu.be/NjBhyGoctwY.

Working with a 4-digit 7-segment display

After learning how to use a shift register with a 7-segment display, we are going to explore how to apply a shift register on a 4-digit 7-segment display. In general, a 4-digit 7-segment display consists of four 7-segment display modules. You can see this module scheme in the following figure (source: http://www.g-nor.com/html/GNQ-5643Ax-Bx.pdf):

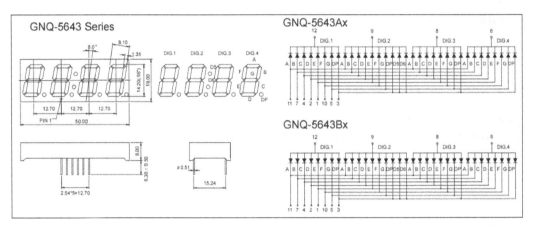

You can see that four 7-segment display modules have been connected and shared on *a*, *b*, *c*, *d*, *f*, *g*, and *DP* pins. To display the first digit on 7-segment, you can set a value *high* on digit-1 (DIG 1). Otherwise, you can display the second digit on 7-segment by setting a value *high* on digit-2 (DIG 2). It means only one 7-segment display is running. You can run all 7-segment displays by manipulating the delay shown on this module.

For a sample illustration, you can see how to display a 4-digit number on this module. To achieve this, we need two 74HC595 shift registers. These chips are formed as cascading shift registers. By cascading two 74HC595 shift registers, we can control 16 bits using three pins. You can build this wiring with the following:

- The segment output (*Q0*, *Q1*, *Q3*, *Q4*, *Q5*, *Q6*, and *Q7*) pins of the first 74HC595 are connected to the segment pins of the 4-digit 7-segment module
- On the first 74HC595, you connect the *Q7* (pin 9) to the *DS* pin (pin 14) from the second 74HC595
- Connect the *STCP* pin (pin 12) from the first 74HC595 to the second one
- Connect the *SHCP* pin (pin 11) from the first 74HC595 to the second one
- *Q0*, *Q1*, *Q2*, and *Q3* pins from the second 74HC595 are connected to digit-1, digit-2, digit-3, and digit-4 pins from the 4-digit 7-segment module

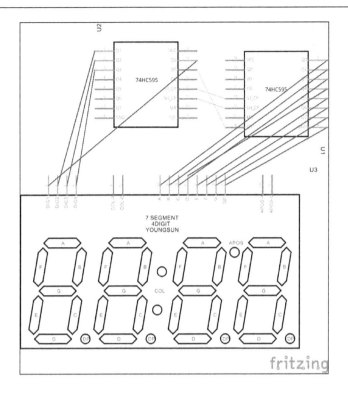

You can also use the 4-digit 7-segment display module with two 74HC595 shift registers easily. For instance, you can get this module on eBay (http://www.ebay. com/itm/291244187011) or Amazon (http://www.amazon.com/Digital-Display- Module-Board-Arduino/dp/B00W9J08I4/). This module uses a 7-segment common anode.

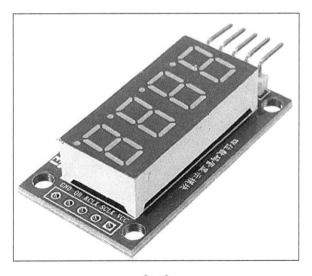

Connect the *DS/Data*, *STCP/LATCH*, and *SHCP/Clock* pins from the first 74HC595 to Raspberry Pi *GPIO25* (wPi 6), *GPIO24* (wPi 5), and *GPIO23* (wPi 4).

After this, we write a program to display a 4-digit number. I have ported and modified code from `http://www.instructables.com/id/74HC595-digital-LED-Display-Based-on-Arduino-Code-/`, so the program can run on Raspberry Pi using Python with the WiringPi library. Create a file, named `ch02_04.py`, and write the following complete code:

```
# ch02_04.py file

import wiringpi2 as wiringpi
import time

# initialize
wiringpi.wiringPiSetup()   # WiPi mode

# define shift reg pins
DATA = 6
LATCH = 5
CLK = 4

OUTPUT = 1
LOW = 0
HIGH = 1

# common anode digital tube 16 BCD code
LED_BCD = [0xc0, 0xf9, 0xa4, 0xb0, 0x99, 0x92, 0x82, 0xf8, 0x80, 0x90,
0x88, 0x83, 0xc6, 0xa1, 0x86, 0x8e]

wiringpi.pinMode(DATA, OUTPUT)
wiringpi.pinMode(LATCH, OUTPUT)
wiringpi.pinMode(CLK, OUTPUT)

# initialization
print("Initialization...")
wiringpi.digitalWrite(LATCH, LOW)
wiringpi.digitalWrite(CLK, LOW)


def LED_display(LED_number, LED_display, LED_dp):
    hc_ledcode_temp = 0
```

```python
    if LED_display > 15:
        LED_display = 0

    hc_ledcode = LED_BCD[LED_display]
    for i in range(0, 8):
        hc_ledcode_temp <<= 1
        if hc_ledcode & 0x01:
            hc_ledcode_temp |= 0x01

        hc_ledcode >>= 1

    if LED_dp:
        hc_ledcode_temp &= 0xfe

    hc_disp = hc_ledcode_temp
    if LED_number == 0:
        hc_disp |= 0x8000
    elif LED_number == 1:
        hc_disp |= 0x4000
    elif LED_number == 2:
        hc_disp |= 0x2000
    elif LED_number == 3:
        hc_disp |= 0x1000

    write_74HC595_ShiftOUTPUT(hc_disp)


def write_74HC595_ShiftOUTPUT(data_a):

    wiringpi.digitalWrite(LATCH, LOW)
    wiringpi.digitalWrite(CLK, LOW)

    for i in range(0, 16):
        if data_a & 0x0001:
            wiringpi.digitalWrite(DATA, HIGH)
        else:
            wiringpi.digitalWrite(DATA, LOW)

        wiringpi.digitalWrite(CLK, HIGH)
        wiringpi.digitalWrite(CLK, LOW)
        data_a >>= 1
```

```
            wiringpi.digitalWrite(LATCH, HIGH)


    print("Running...")
    try:
        timer = 0
        digit = 0
        while 1:
            LED_display(0, digit, 0)
            time.sleep(0.01)
            LED_display(1, digit, 0)
            time.sleep(0.01)
            LED_display(2, digit, 0)
            time.sleep(0.01)
            LED_display(3, digit, 0)
            time.sleep(0.01)

            timer += 1
            if timer > 10:
                time.sleep(0.05)
                timer = 0
                digit += 1
                if digit > 9:
                    digit = 0

    except KeyboardInterrupt:
        write_74HC595_ShiftOUTPUT(0)

    print("done")
```

Here is the code explanation:

- Declare the LED_BCD variable for a collection of **Binary-Coded Decimal (BCD)** values, so you map 7-segment values to binary ones; for instance, digit-1 can be constructed as 0x11000000. In this scenario, we just pass a value 1, not 0x11000000 to display digit-1.

- Declare the LED_display (LED_number, LED_display, LED_dp) function to display a number on a specific digit. This function is used to parse input data. Then, call the write_74HC595() function to display it on the 7-segment module. LED_number is a digit position. The value could be 0, 1, 2, or 4 for 4-digit 7-segments. LED_display is a digit number that will be displayed on the 7-segment display. LED_dp will show whether there is a digit dot or not.

- Declare the `write_74HC595_ShiftOUTPUT()` function to show a number on the module. It starts by sending data into the *DATA* pin and then sends a *Clock* signal. After 16 bits are sent to the *DATA* pin, we push this data into the 74HC595 IC's storage by sending a *LATCH* signal.

- The program will display a number from 0 to 9 on all digit modules.

- Set a delay via `time.sleep()`, so it seems as though the 4-digit panels appear together.

There are four digits on this module. So if we want four digits to be displayed simultaneously, we do a trick by adding a delay. The following is my approach to displaying a delay:

```
timer += 1
if timer > 10:
    time.sleep(0.05)
    timer = 0
    digit += 1
    if digit > 9:
        digit = 0
```

Save this file. Now you can run the program by typing the following command:

`sudo python ch02_04.py`

If this gets success, you should see a number on each digit module. You can also see this demonstration in my YouTube, `http://youtu.be/yvciVugNnS0`.

Building a countdown timer

In the previous section, we already learned how to display four digits on a 7-segment module and wrote the program for displaying a 4-digit number (`ch02_04.py`). In this section, we continue to build a simple program for a countdown timer using a 4-digit 7-segment module and two 74HC595 shift registers.

Our scenario is to get a number input from the user, for instance, 30. After this, the number is displayed on the module. Then, we decrease the number down to 0.

Let's copy the `ch02_04.py` file and then modify it as follows:

```
# ch02_05.py
...

...
print("Running...")
number_s = raw_input("Enter a number (1-999): ")
number = int(number_s)
```

```python
print("Countdown " + number_s)
try:
    timer = 0

    while 1:
        digit = number

        LED_display(0, digit % 10, 0)
        digit /= 10
        time.sleep(0.01)

        LED_display(1, digit % 10, 0)
        time.sleep(0.01)
        digit /= 10

        LED_display(2, digit % 10, 0)
        time.sleep(0.01)
        digit /= 10

        LED_display(3, digit, 0)
        time.sleep(0.01)

        timer += 1
        if timer > 10:
            time.sleep(0.05)
            timer = 0
            number -= 1
            if number < 0:
                write_74HC595_ShiftOUTPUT(0)
                break

except KeyboardInterrupt:
    write_74HC595_ShiftOUTPUT(0)
print("done")
```

Save this program in a file named ch02_05.py. You can run it by typing the following command on the terminal.

```
sudo python ch02_05.py
```

Enter a number, for instance, 50. After this, you should see the number decrementing. You can see this demonstration in my YouTube, http://youtu.be/11FM1SsSn3Y.

```
pi@raspberrypi ~/led $ sudo python ch02_05.py
Initialization...
Running...
Enter a number (1-999): 50
Countdown 50
done
pi@raspberrypi ~/led $ ▮
```

In general, this program works like the previous program, ch02_04.py. After obtaining input data from a user, we display it on digit-1, digit-2, digit-3, and digit-4. It uses a modulo operation. Please read it at https://docs.python.org/2/reference/expressions.html#binary-arithmetic-operations. For instance, if the input data is 2456, the program will do the following steps:

1. Digit-0 displays a unit with formula digit % 10, and the result is **6**.
2. Digit-1 displays **5**.
3. Digit-2 displays **4**.
4. Digit-1 displays **2**.
5. After displaying the number for a specific duration, the number is decremented and returns to step 1.

Summary

Let's summarize what we have learned in this chapter. We connected a 7-segment module to a Raspberry Pi board through eight GPIO pins. Then, we show a number on the module. To minimize the GPIO pin usage, we implemented a shift register using a 74HC595 IC, so we only need three GPIO pins. A shift register is also used to drive a 4-digit 7-segment module by cascading two 74HC595 shift registers. At the end of the section, we tried to build a simple program for a countdown timer.

In the next chapter, we will build a digital clock using several LED modules. The chapter will introduce LED modules related to the digital clock stack.

3

Make Your Own Digital Clock Display

We explore how to build a digital clock in this chapter. A digital clock is a type of clock that displays the time digitally. In general, it uses four digits of which two digits are used as the hour display and the rest are used as the minute display. First, we use a 4-digit 7-segment display module. Then, we introduce an OLED graphic display with an I2C interface and describe how to use it to build a digital clock.

You will learn the following topics in this chapter:

- Introducing a 4-digit 7-segment display for a digital clock
- Introducing an I2C OLED graphic display
- Building a digital clock using an I2C OLED graphic display

Introducing a 4-digit 7-segment display for a digital clock

In *Chapter 2, Make Your Own Countdown Timer*, we learned how to use a 4-digit 7-segment display and build it as a countdown counter. Now we try to build a digital clock using this module. The algorithm for displaying a digital clock is easy, and is as follows:

- Initialize Raspberry Pi GPIO
- Perform a looping process

- In the looping process, you do the following tasks:
    - Read the current time
    - Extract the minute value and then change the minute value on the module
    - Extract the hour value and then change the hour value on the module

Let's start to implement a digital clock using a 4-digit 7-segment display. We use a 4-digit 7-segment display with two 74HC595 shift registers. We can obtain it on eBay, `http://www.ebay.com/itm/291244187011`. We can also obtain it on Amazon, `http://www.amazon.com/Digital-Display-Module-Board-Arduino/dp/B00W9J08I4/`.

Connect the *DS/Data, STCP/LATCH*, and *SHCP/Clock* pins from the first 74HC595 to Raspberry Pi *GPIO25* (wPi 6), *GPIO24* (wPi 5), and *GPIO23* (wPi 4).

Then, we modify the `ch02_04.py` file. We change the code in the main program. Write the following code:

```
// ch03_01.py

print("Demo - digital clock")
print("Running....")
print("Press CTRL-C to exit....")
try:

    while 1:
        # get current time
        now = datetime.datetime.now()
        minute = now.minute
        hour = now.hour

        # display minute
        LED_display(0, minute % 10, 0)
        minute /= 10
        time.sleep(0.01)
        LED_display(1, minute, 0)
        time.sleep(0.01)
```

```
            # display hour
            LED_display(2, hour % 10, 1)
            hour /= 10
            time.sleep(0.01)
            LED_display(3, hour, 0)
            time.sleep(0.01)

    except KeyboardInterrupt:
        write_74HC595_ShiftOUTPUT(0)

    print("done")
```

Save this code in a file named ch03_01.py.

Now you can run this file by typing the following command:

`sudo python ch03_01.py`

If it is successful, the module shows a digital clock. It changes on minute and hour values. This demo can be seen on YouTube, http://youtu.be/oP_13g7asx8.

```
pi@raspberrypi ~/led $ sudo python ch03_01.py
Initialization...
Demo - digital clock
Running....
Press CTRL-C to exit....
```

Introducing an I2C OLED graphic display

We can display a digital clock using an OLED graphic display module. **OLED** stands for **organic light-emitting diode**. The OLED display is made up of organic compounds that light up when fed electricity. If you have any experience with LED backlighting and LCD display, an OLED display can be controlled pixel by pixel. This sort of control just isn't possible with an LED and LCD.

There are many models of OLED graphic display. You can review them at
`https://www.adafruit.com/categories/98`. In this section, we will learn to
build a digital clock using a Monochrome 0.96" 128 x 64 OLED graphic display.
You can buy it on `https://www.adafruit.com/products/326` and you can also
get it on eBay at low cost. To access an OLED module, we use an I2C protocol on
Raspberry Pi:

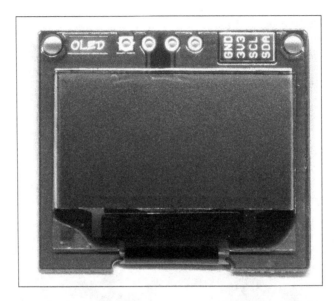

The I2C OLED graphic display has the following pinouts: *GND*, *3V3*, *SCL*, and *SDA*.
These pinouts match with your Raspberry Pi I2C.

The **I2C (Inter-IC)** bus is a bidirectional two-wire serial bus that provides a
communication link between **integrated circuits (ICs)**. This OLED display module
uses I2C to control what we want to show. It is assumed that you will understand
about I2C protocols, but if you don't have experience with I2C, please read this
topic on the Sparkfun website, `https://learn.sparkfun.com/tutorials/i2c`.

Enabling I2C on Raspberry Pi

By default, Raspberry Pi disables the I2C port. Therefore, if we want to access the I2C
port, we must active it via `raspi-config`. Type the following command:

```
sudo raspi-config
```

You should get a `raspi-config` form. Select **Advanced Options,** as shown in the following screenshot:

```
ââââââââââ¤ Raspberry Pi Software Configuration Tool (raspi-config) ââââââââââââ
â                                                                            â
â      1 Expand Filesystem           Ensures that all of the SD card s        â
â      2 Change User Password        Change password for the default u        â
â      3 Enable Boot to Desktop/Scratch Choose whether to boot into a des     â
â      4 Internationalisation Options Set up language and regional sett       â
â      5 Enable Camera               Enable this Pi to work with the R        â
â      6 Add to Rastrack             Add this Pi to the online Raspber        â
â      7 Overclock                   Configure overclocking for your P        â
â      8 Advanced Options            Configure advanced settings              â
â      9 About raspi-config          Information about this configurat        â
â                                                                            â
â                                                                            â
â                                                                            â
â                  <Select>                      <Finish>                    â
â                                                                            â
ââââââââââââââââââââââââââââââââââââââââââââââââââââââââââââââââââââââââââââââââ
```

After selecting **Advanced Options**, you get a list of configuration menus. Please select **A7 I2C**. Then, activate it by enabling this port. Click the **Finish** button when done:

```
ââââââââââ¤ Raspberry Pi Software Configuration Tool (raspi-config) ââââââââââââ
â                                                                            â
â      A1 Overscan                You may need to configure oversca           â
â      A2 Hostname                Set the visible name for this Pi            â
â      A3 Memory Split            Change the amount of memory made            â
â      A4 SSH                     Enable/Disable remote command lin           â
â      A5 Device Tree             Enable/Disable the use of Device            â
â      A6 SPI                     Enable/Disable automatic loading            â
â      A7 I2C                     Enable/Disable automatic loading            â
â      A8 Serial                  Enable/Disable shell and kernel m           â
â      A9 Audio                   Force audio out through HDMI or 3           â
â      A0 Update                  Update this tool to the latest ve           â
â                                                                            â
â                                                                            â
â                  <Select>                      <Back>                      â
â                                                                            â
ââââââââââââââââââââââââââââââââââââââââââââââââââââââââââââââââââââââââââââââââ
```

After finishing, Raspbian loads the I2C module automatically when starting up. You can verify this by checking the `/boot/config.txt` file. You should see **dtparam=i2c_arm=on**.

Another approach to forcing our Raspian OS to load the I2C module into the kernel is to open the /etc/modules file and add the following script:

```
i2c-bcm2708
i2c-dev
```

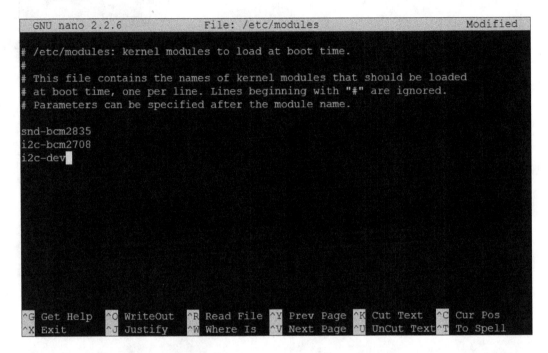

```
  GNU nano 2.2.6              File: /etc/modules                    Modified

# /etc/modules: kernel modules to load at boot time.
#
# This file contains the names of kernel modules that should be loaded
# at boot time, one per line. Lines beginning with "#" are ignored.
# Parameters can be specified after the module name.

snd-bcm2835
i2c-bcm2708
i2c-dev






^G Get Help   ^O WriteOut   ^R Read File  ^Y Prev Page  ^K Cut Text   ^C Cur Pos
^X Exit       ^J Justify    ^W Where Is   ^V Next Page  ^U UnCut Text ^T To Spell
```

If you are running Raspian OS with a 3.18 kernel or higher, you need to update the /boot/config.txt file. Edit it with sudo nano /boot/config.txt and add the following text:

```
dtparam=i2c1=on
dtparam=i2c_arm=on
```

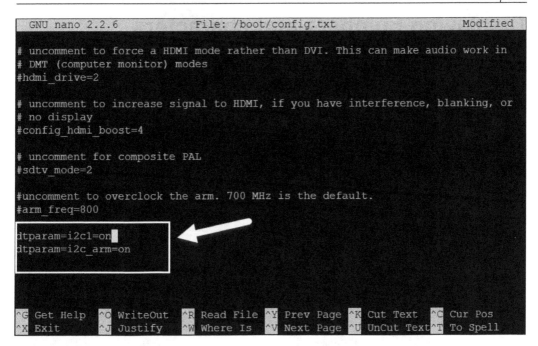

When you have finished all these tasks, you should reboot your Raspberry Pi with the following command:

```
sudo reboot
```

The I2C library for Python

In *Chapter 1, Getting Started with LED Programming through Raspberry Pi GPIO*, we already used WiringPi for Python available at `https://github.com/Gadgetoid/WiringPi2-Python`. This library provides an I2C module for accessing the I2C protocol. It is assumed that you have already installed `https://github.com/Gadgetoid/WiringPi2-Python`. You also need I2C tools. Type the following commands:

```
sudo apt-get install python-smbus
sudo apt-get install i2c-tools
```

You're ready to develop a program-based I2C!

Displaying numbers and characters

To illustrate how to use an I2C port, we use an OLED graphic display module. Connect it to Raspberry Pi I2C. Read the I2C port location from the GPIO pins from *Chapter 1, Started with LED Programming through Raspberry Pi GPIO*.

The following is the wiring for displaying numbers and characters on OLED graphic display:

After all the components are connected, you can verify it by typing the following command:

```
sudo i2cdetect -y 1
```

If it is successful, you should see the OLED I2C address. By default, it has an I2C address on 0 x 3C. To implement I2C on a 128 x 64 OLED graphic display, we can use the `lib_oled96` library, which is available at `https://github.com/BLavery/lib_oled96`.

```
pi@raspberrypi ~ $ sudo i2cdetect -y 1
     0  1  2  3  4  5  6  7  8  9  a  b  c  d  e  f
00:          -- -- -- -- -- -- -- -- -- -- -- -- --
10: -- -- -- -- -- -- -- -- -- -- -- -- -- -- -- --
20: -- -- -- -- -- -- -- -- -- -- -- -- -- -- -- --
30: -- -- -- -- -- -- -- -- -- -- -- -- 3c -- -- --
40: -- -- -- -- -- -- -- -- -- -- -- -- -- -- -- --
50: -- -- -- -- -- -- -- -- -- -- -- -- -- -- -- --
60: -- -- -- -- -- -- -- -- -- -- -- -- -- -- -- --
70: -- -- -- -- -- -- -- --
pi@raspberrypi ~ $
```

First, we download the `lib_oled96.py` file from `https://github.com/BLavery/lib_oled96`. Type the following command:

```
wget
https://raw.githubusercontent.com/BLavery/lib_oled96/master/lib_oled96
.py
```

You also need a **python-imaging library** (PIL) on Raspbian. You can get it by typing the following command on a terminal:

```
sudo apt-get install python-imaging
```

Furthermore, we write our program to display numbers and characters. Create a file, named `ch03_02.py`. Write the following scripts:

```
# ch03_02.py file

from lib_oled96 import ssd1306
from smbus import SMBus

i2cbus = SMBus(1)
oled = ssd1306(i2cbus)


# put border around the screen:
oled.canvas.rectangle((0, 0, oled.width-1, oled.height-1), outline=1,
fill=0)
```

```
# Write two lines of text.
oled.canvas.text((15,15),     'Hello World, Pi!!', fill=1)
oled.canvas.text((30,30),     '123456780%!&', fill=1)

# now display that canvas out to the hardware
oled.display()
```

Here is the code explanation:

- Initialize I2C port using SMBus
- Draw a rectangle using `canvas.rectangle()`
- Show some text using `canvas.text()`

Then, you can execute it by typing the following command:

```
sudo python ch03_02.py
```

You should see **Hello World, Pi!!** and **123456780%!&** on the OLED graphic display, as shown in the following figure:

You can find this demo uploaded on YouTube, `http://youtu.be/M6fIv5f45Z0`. You can see the demo output.

Building a digital clock using an I2C OLED graphic display

We have already learned how to use an I2C OLED graphic display. The next step is to build a digital clock using this module. In this scenario, we show hours and minutes on an OLED graphic display. If the minute or hour value changes from the current time on Raspberry Pi, we update the values on the OLED graphic display.

In addition, we need a font file to display numbers on the OLED graphic display. Download the FreeSans.ttf file using the following command:

```
wget
https://raw.githubusercontent.com/BLavery/lib_oled96/master/FreeSans.
ttf
```

To open a font file, we need the PIL library. Type the following command to install it:

```
sudo apt-get install python-imaging
```

Now we can write our program. Create a file, named ch03_03.py, and write the following complete code:

```python
# ch03_03.py file

from lib_oled96 import ssd1306
from smbus import SMBus
from PIL import ImageFont
import datetime


i2cbus = SMBus(1)
oled = ssd1306(i2cbus)
draw = oled.canvas

font = ImageFont.load_default()
font = ImageFont.truetype('FreeSans.ttf', 48)
draw.rectangle((0, 0, oled.width-1, oled.height-1), outline=1, fill=0)
oled.display()

def show_clock(text):
    global oled
    global draw
    global font
```

```
    draw.rectangle((5, 5, oled.width-5, oled.height-8), outline=0,
fill=0)
    draw.text((5, 5), text, font=font, fill=1)
    oled.display()


print("Demo - digital clock")
print("Running....")
print("Press CTRL-C to exit....")

try:
    counter = 0
    minute = -1
    bar = 2
    while 1:
        # get current time
        now = datetime.datetime.now()
        temp_min = now.minute
        hour = now.hour
        temp = now.second
        str = ""
        if temp_min!=minute:
            # change time
            minute = temp_min
            str = now.strftime("%H:%M")
            show_clock(str)

        counter += 1
        if counter > 10:
            draw.rectangle((1, oled.height-6,  bar, oled.height-3),
outline=1, fill=0)
            oled.display()
            bar += 1
            counter = 0
            if bar > 127:
                draw.rectangle((1, oled.height-6,  bar-2, oled.
height-3), outline=0, fill=0)
                oled.display()
                bar = 2


except KeyboardInterrupt:
    oled.onoff(0)
    oled.cls()

print("done")
```

The code explanation is as follows:

- Initialize I2C port using SMBus
- Initialize the `lib_oled96` library
- Load a font file using `ImageFont.truetype()`
- Define the `show_clock()` function to display text
- Read the current time
- Updating the minute or hour value if its value changes
- Draw a moving rectangle from left to right

Save this code. Then execute it on the terminal using the following command:

```
sudo python ch03_03.py
```

If successful, you should see a digital clock with the current time on the OLED graphic display. A moving line also can be seen on the OLED display. A sample output can be seen in the following figure:

This demonstartion is available on YouTube, `http://youtu.be/0FlmgrArntk`, so you can see the demo output.

Summary

We used the 4-digit 7-segment module to display a digital clock on a Raspberry Pi board via a shift register. Furthermore, we studied an OLED graphic display module, which can be accessed through an I2C port. The last topic is to use the OLED graphic display to develop a digital clock.

In the next chapter, we will learn how to build several applications with an LED dot matrix (8 x 8 LEDs). There are some project scenarios to illustrate how it works.

4

LED Dot Matrix

An LED dot matrix display is a two-dimensional LED pattern array, used to represent characters, symbols, and images. This chapter will explore how to control an LED dot matrix display from Raspberry Pi. At the end of the chapter, we will cascade several LED dot matrix modules.

You will learn the following topics in this chapter:

- Introducing LED dot matrix display (8 x 8 LEDs)
- Displaying a random number in an LED dot matrix display
- Displaying a random character in an LED dot matrix display
- Building a ball reflection game
- Cascading LED dot matrix modules

Introducing LED dot matrix display (8 x 8 LEDs)

In the previous chapter, you learned how to build a digital clock using 4-digit 7-segment and OLED display modules. In this chapter, we will learn how to work with an LED dot matrix display and focus on 8 x 8 LEDs' model. These LEDs can have monochrome color or RGB color. To simplify the problem, we will use monochrome color on the LED dot matrix display module.

In an LED matrix display, multiple LEDs are connected together in row and columns. This connection is established to reduce the number of pins needed to manipulate them. For instance, the 8 x 8 LED dot matrix is shown in the following figure:

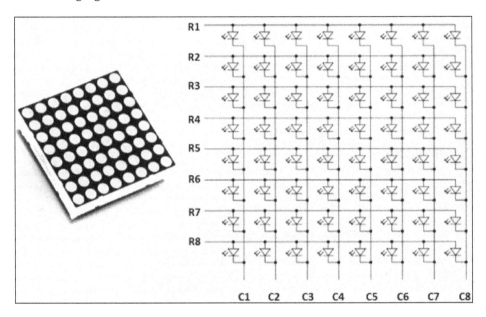

In the preceding figure, if R3 is in 1 logic and C2 is in 0 logic, the LED on line 3 column 3 will be turned on. The characters will be displayed by fast scanning each row and column. For illustration, if we need to display the character **A**, we can draw the following figure on our dot matrix:

	C1	C2	C3	C4	C5	C6	C7	C8
R1	0	0	1	1	1	1	0	0
R2	0	0	1	1	1	1	0	0
R3	0	1	0	0	0	0	1	0
R4	0	1	0	0	0	0	1	0
R5	0	1	1	1	1	1	1	0
R6	0	1	0	0	0	0	1	0
R7	0	1	0	0	0	0	1	0
R8	0	0	0	0	0	0	0	0
	C1	C2	C3	C4	C5	C6	C7	C8
HEX	00	3E	C8	C8	C8	C8	3E	00

An MCU, which wants to work with 8 x 8 LED dot matrix display module, needs at least 16 GPIO pins. To reduce the number of pins, we need an LED dot matrix display. You will be introduced to one of the LED dot matrix drivers, applied IC MAX7219.

Some online electronics stores provide dot matrix display including a driver with MAX7219. You can obtain this module at the following stores:

- Sparkfun, `https://www.sparkfun.com/products/11861`

- Banggood, `http://www.banggood.com/MAX7219-Dot-Matrix-Module-DIY-Kit-SCM-Control-Module-For-Arduino-p-72178.html`

- Linksprite, `http://store.linksprite.com/max7219-8x8-red-dot-led-matrix-kit/`

- eBay, `http://www.ebay.com`

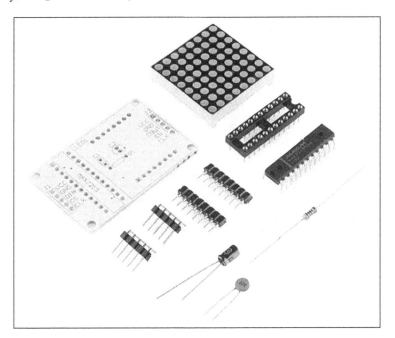

For testing, we use an LED dot matrix module with a 7219 driver. You can buy this module from eBay. The dot matrix display is connected to IC MAX7219 and has the *VCC*, *GND*, *DIN*, *CS*, and *CLK* output pins.

 For further information about IC MAX7219, you can read its datasheet at `http://datasheets.maximintegrated.com/en/ds/MAX7219-MAX7221.pdf`.

In general, we can attach this module through the **Serial Peripheral Interface (SPI)** port. In SPI, only one side generates the clock signal (*CLK* or *SCK*), and usually called the **master**, and the other side is called the **slave**. SPI has four lines: *SCK*, *MOSI* (Master Out / Slave In), and *MISO* (Master In / Slave Out). I will explain in the next section how to enable SPI on Raspberry Pi. The following is the testing module for this:

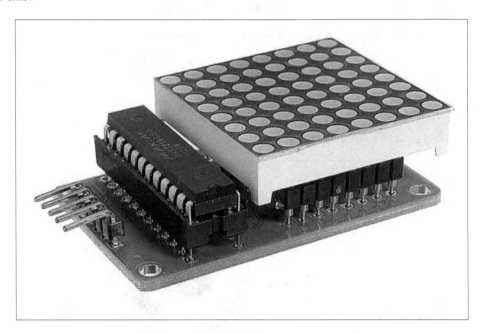

Introducing an LED dot matrix driver

Richard Hull and his team have already built an LED dot matrix driver based on IC MAX7219. You can download it from `https://github.com/rm-hull/max7219`. This library also supports cascading several dot matrix display modules. This means that we can cascade several LED dot matrix modules by connecting *DOUT* to *DIN* among these modules. You will learn how to cascade LED dot matrix modules in the last section of this chapter.

The library needs the SPI library to run the LED dot matrix display module. In the next section, I'm going to explain how to activate SPI on a Raspberry Pi board.

Enabling Raspberry Pi SPI

By default, Raspberry Pi disables the SPI port, so if we want to access the SPI port, we must activate it via `raspi-config`. Type the following command:

```
sudo raspi-config
```

You should get a `raspi-config` form. Select **Advanced Options**. Then, you should select **A6 SPI**, as shown in the following screenshot. Confirm to enable and load SPI onto Raspberry Pi. The setup tool will ask for enabling to load the SPI module automatically. Please click **Yes** to confirm:

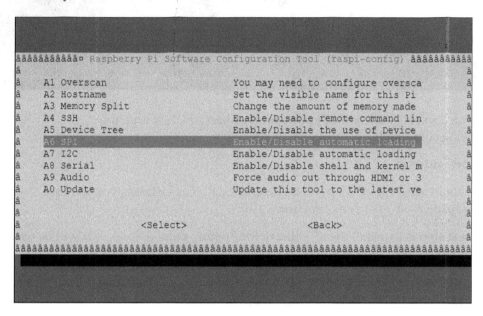

After this, you will need to reboot your Raspberry Pi. Now you can verify whether the SPI library has loaded or not. Please type the following command:

```
lsmod
```

If successful, you should see that **spi_bcm2708** is loaded as shown here:

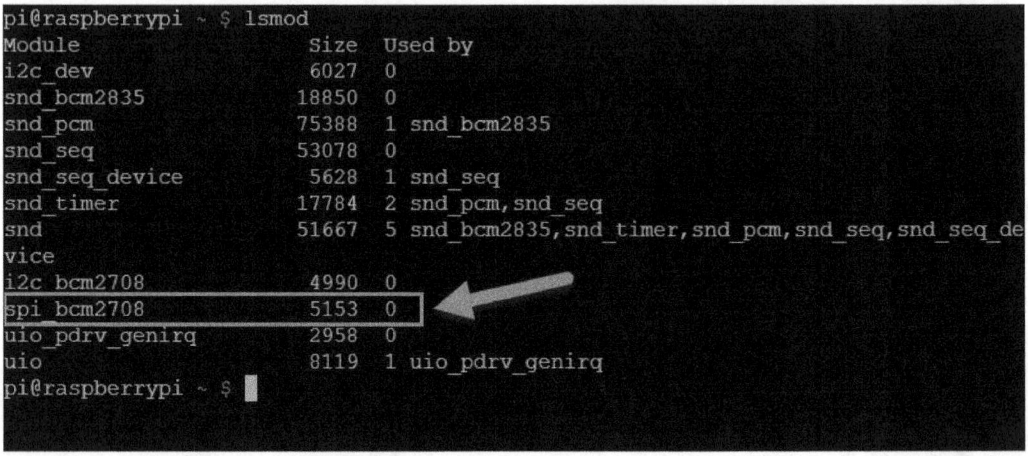

```
pi@raspberrypi ~ $ lsmod
Module                 Size  Used by
i2c_dev                6027  0
snd_bcm2835           18850  0
snd_pcm               75388  1 snd_bcm2835
snd_seq               53078  0
snd_seq_device         5628  1 snd_seq
snd_timer             17784  2 snd_pcm,snd_seq
snd                   51667  5 snd_bcm2835,snd_timer,snd_pcm,snd_seq,snd_seq_de
vice
i2c_bcm2708            4990  0
spi_bcm2708            5153  0
uio_pdrv_genirq        2958  0
uio                    8119  1 uio_pdrv_genirq
pi@raspberrypi ~ $
```

You can also check a list of SPI ports on Raspberry Pi. Just type the following command:

```
ls /dev/spidev*
```

You should see a list of SPI ports on Raspberry Pi. For instance, you may see `/dev/spidev0.0` and `/dev/spidev0.1`.

The next step is to install the SPI library for Python, named `spidev`. It will be used in our program. You can install it by typing the following commands:

```
sudo apt-get install python-dev python-pip
sudo pip install spidev
```

Your Raspberry is ready for SPI programming using Python.

Deploying a matrix 7219 driver

To install a matrix 7219 driver from `https://github.com/rm-hull/max7219`, you can download it and then install it. Type the following commands on terminal:

```
git clone https://github.com/rm-hull/max7219
cd max7219
sudo python setup.py install
```

We need to test this library using a 8 x 8 LED dot matrix display with the MAX7219 driver. The following is our wiring:

- The *VCC* module is connected to *VCC* +5 V Raspberry Pi
- The *GND* module is connected to *GND* +5 V Raspberry Pi
- The *DIN* module is connected to *GPIO10* (MOSI) Raspberry Pi
- The *CS* module is connected to *GPIO8* (SPI CE0) Raspberry Pi
- The *CLK* module is connected to *GPIO11* (SPI CLK) Raspberry Pi

Our testing scenario is to display the character **A** on an 8 x 8 LED dot matrix display. Create a Python file named ch04_01.py. Write the following:

```
# ch04_01.py file

import max7219.led as led
import time


print("Running...")
print("Display character A")

device = led.matrix(cascaded=1)
device.letter(0, ord('A'))

raw_input("Press Enter to exit ")
device.command(led.constants.MAX7219_REG_SHUTDOWN,0x00)
time.sleep(0.01)
```

Here is the code explanation:

- Load the max7219.led library using the import syntax.
- Initialize the matrix object from the Max7219 library and set cascading as *1*. It's required if you are using one LED matrix module. If you want to work with several LED matrix modules, you can read the last section of this chapter.
- Display the character **A** using the letter (self, deviceId, asciiCode, font=None, redraw=True) function. Since we have one LED dot matrix module, we set deviceId = 0. We need asciiCode for input, and we can use the ord() function to convert from a character to ASCII code.

Save this code and execute this file. Type the following command:

```
sudo python ch04_01.py
```

You should see the character **A** on the dot matrix module. A sample output can be seen in the following figure:

You can also see it on YouTube at `http://youtu.be/fP_weX2PVcg`. On the terminal, you should see the program output, as shown in the following figure:

```
pi@raspberrypi ~/led $ sudo python ch04_01.py
Running...
Display character A
Press Enter to exit
pi@raspberrypi ~/led $
```

Displaying a random number on the LED dot matrix display

In this section, we will explore more practices using 8 x 8 LED dot matrix displays. We will display a random number on the LED dot matrix module. A number will be generated by a Python program via random object and then shown on the LED dot matrix display.

Let's start to write the program. Create a file named ch04_02.py. Write the following completed code:

```
# ch04_02.py file

import max7219.led as led
import time
```

```
import random

device = led.matrix(cascaded=1)

print("Running...")
print("Press CTRL+C to exit ")
try:
    while 1:
        number = random.randint(0,9)
        print "display ", number
        device.letter(0, ord(str(number)))
        time.sleep(1)

except KeyboardInterrupt:
    device.command(led.constants.MAX7219_REG_SHUTDOWN,0x00)
    time.sleep(0.01)

print("done")
```

We can generate a random number by using random.randint() from random object.
We pass (0,9) so it generates value from 0 to 9. After this, we pass this random
number into the device.letter() function, which needs ASCII code parameters, so
we use the ord() function to convert by using input to ASCII code. Since the number
is number data type, we change it to string by using the str() function.

Save this program. Now you will can execute this program by typing the
following command:

sudo python ch04_02.py

If successful, you can see a random number on the 8 x 8 LED dot matrix display,
as shown in the following screenshot:

This demo can be seen on YouTube at `ttp://youtu.be/ZDCighD1p3s`. You should also see the output from the program as follows:

```
pi@raspberrypi ~/led $ sudo python ch04_02.py
Running...
Press CTRL+C to exit
display  6
display  7
display  9
display  9
display  7
display  1
display  1
display  4
display  5
display  3
display  0
display  8
display  7
display  4
display  2
```

Displaying a random character on the LED dot matrix display

Using the scenario from the previous section, we can build a simple program to display a random character on an 8 x 8 LED dot matrix module. We can use `random.choice(string.ascii_letters)` to retrieve a random character in Python. After this, the random value is passed to the MAX7219 library.

Let's start. Create a file named `ch04_03.py`. The following is completed code for our scenario:

```
# ch04_03.py file

import max7219.led as led
import time
import random
import string

device = led.matrix(cascaded=1)
```

```
print("Running...")
print("Press CTRL+C to exit ")
try:
    while 1:
        character = random.choice(string.ascii_letters)
        print "display ", character
        device.letter(0, ord(character))
        time.sleep(1)

except KeyboardInterrupt:
    device.command(led.constants.MAX7219_REG_SHUTDOWN,0x00)
    time.sleep(0.01)

print("done")
```

Save this code. Execute this program by typing the following command:

`sudo python ch04_03.py`

You should see a random character on the 8 x 8 LED dot matrix display, as shown in the following screenshot:

This demo can be seen on YouTube at http://youtu.be/zjsVKtiP6ug.
On the terminal, you should also see the output from the program,
as shown in the following screenshot:

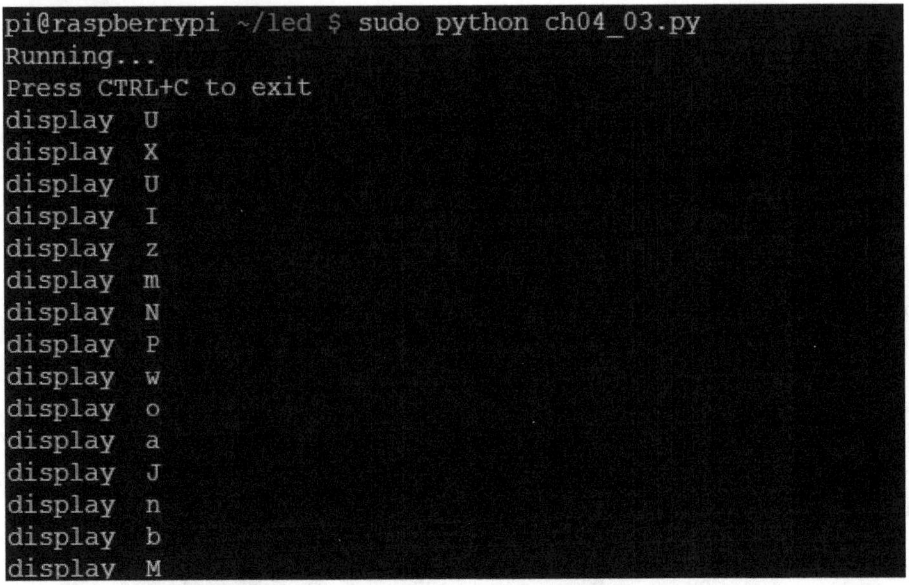

```
pi@raspberrypi ~/led $ sudo python ch04_03.py
Running...
Press CTRL+C to exit
display  U
display  X
display  U
display  I
display  z
display  m
display  N
display  P
display  w
display  o
display  a
display  J
display  n
display  b
display  M
```

Building a ball reflection game

A dot matrix display module consists of LEDs. Each LED can act as a pixel and can
be used as a ball. In this section, we build a ball reflection game. If a ball hits a corner,
it will bounce back. The ball can move with a specific speed, which is extracted
as horizontal speed (vx) and vertical speed (vy). The following is the formula for
moving the ball:

```
pos_x = pos_x + (vx * direction)
pos_y = pos_y + (vy * direction)
```

This formula uses object moving-based vectors with speeds vx and vy direction is a
direction orientation. If the direction value is *1*, the ball will move from left to right.
Otherwise, it will move from right to left.

Let's start to build a program. Create a file named ch04_04.py. Write the following completed code:

```
# ch04_04.py file

import max7219.led as led
import time


device = led.matrix(cascaded=1)

# you can change these initial data
pos_x = 4   # current position x
pos_y = 4   # current position y
last_x = pos_x # last position x
last_y = pos_y # last position y
vx = 1 # speed x
vy = 2 # speed y


def draw_ball():
    global pos_x
    global pos_y
    global last_x
    global last_y

    device.pixel(last_x, last_y, 0)
    last_x = pos_x
    last_y = pos_y
    device.pixel(pos_x, pos_y, 1)


def validate_position():
    global pos_x
    global pos_y

    if pos_x > 7:
        pos_x = 7
    if pos_y > 7:
        pos_y = 7
    if pos_x < 0:
        pos_x = 0
    if pos_y < 0:
        pos_y = 0
```

```
# show ball first
device.pixel(pos_x,pos_y,1)
time.sleep(1)
direction = 1

print("Running...")
print("Press CTRL+C to exit ")
try:
    while 1:
        pos_x = pos_x + (vx * direction)
        pos_y = pos_y + (vy * direction)

        validate_position()
        draw_ball()

        # change direction
        if pos_x >= 7:
            direction = -1
        if pos_x <= 0:
            direction = 1

        time.sleep(1)

except KeyboardInterrupt:
    device.command(led.constants.MAX7219_REG_SHUTDOWN,0x00)
    time.sleep(0.01)

print("done")
```

Here is the explanation:

- First, define the initial position and speed
- Set the ball speed $vx = 1$ and $vy = 2$
- A ball moves by adding its position to the current position with vx and vy
- Define the `draw_ball()` function to draw a ball on the 8 x 8 dot matrix display based on the current position of ball

Since the 8 x 8 LED dot matrix display has eight points, we should validate the `pos_x` and `pos_y` values with the following validation:

```
if pos_x >= 7:
    direction = -1
if pos_x <= 0:
    direction = 1
```

This code uses global variables. You can read another approach to use local variables for pos_x, pos_y, last_x, and last_y. Please open the ch04_o4b.py file.

Save this code. Execute the program by typing the following command:

```
sudo python ch04_04.py
```

After you execute, you should see a reflecting ball on the 8 x 8 dot matrix display, as shown in the following screenshot:

See the demo on YouTube at http://youtu.be/2MtZbJcP0Ec.

Cascading LED dot matrix modules

Sometimes you want to cascade several LED dot matrix display modules. If you have LED dot matrix display with theMAX7219 driver, it provides *DIN* and *DOUT* pins. These pins are used to cascade our LED dot matrix display.

For instance, we have two 8 x 8 LED dot matrix display modules. The first module is attached to Raspberry Pi as usual. For the second module, connect *DIN* to *DOUT* from the first module. The *CS* and *CLK* pins from the first module are connected to the *CS* and *CLK* pins from the second module.

Please note that if you cascade two 8 x 8 LED dot matrix display modules, the *(0, 0)* position is located on the second LED dot matrix module. The following is the wiring for two cascaded LED dot matrix modules:

- All LED dot matrix *VCC* pins are connected to +5 V Raspberry Pi
- All LED dot matrix *GND* pins are connected to *GND* Raspberry Pi
- The *DOUT* pin from the first LED dot matrix display is connected to the *DIN* pin from the second LED dot matrix display
- The *DIN* pin from the first LED dot matrix display is connected to *GPIO10* (MOSI) Raspberry Pi
- All LED dot matrix *CS* pins are connected to *GPIO8* (SPI CE0) Raspberry Pi
- All LED dot matrix *CLK* pins are connected to *GPIO11* (SPI CLK) Raspberry Pi

For illustration, we build a working ball (a pixel on dot matrix) from *(0, 0)* to *(15, 8)*. As stated, the *(0, 0)* position is located on the second module, so we do a trick. We build the *x* position mapping into an array, `pos_x_list = [8,9,10,11,12,13,14,15,0,1,2,3,4,5,6,7]`. You can see that the position 0 is located on the second module of the LED dot matrix display.

Let's build a program. Create a file named `ch04_05.py`. The following is the completed code:

```
# ch04_05.py file

import max7219.led as led
import time


device = led.matrix(cascaded=2)

pos_x_list =[8,9,10,11,12,13,14,15,0,1,2,3,4,5,6,7]
pos_x = 0
pos_y = 0
direction = 1
print("Running...")
print("Press CTRL+C to cancel ")
try:
    while 1:
```

```
print "x=", pos_x, "  y=",pos_y
device.pixel(pos_x_list[pos_x], pos_y, 1)
time.sleep(0.2)

# clear pixel
device.pixel(pos_x_list[pos_x], pos_y, 0)
pos_x = pos_x + direction
if pos_x > 15:
    pos_y = pos_y + 1
    pos_x = 15
    direction = direction * (-1)

if pos_x < 0:
    pos_y = pos_y + 1
    pos_x = 0
    direction = direction * (-1)

# stop on right-bottom
if pos_y > 7:
    break

except KeyboardInterrupt:
    device.command(led.constants.MAX7219_REG_SHUTDOWN,0x00)
    time.sleep(0.01)

print("done")
```

Here is the explanation:

- Set `cascaded=2` to instantiat process for the matrix object.
- Define `pos_x_list = [8,9,10,11,12,13,14,15,0,1,2,3,4,5,6,7]` as the pin mapping for two modules. For instance, if we move a ball to $x = 0$, our mapping returns `8`.
- Make the ball move by increasing or decreasing the x and y values. You can change these values.

Save this code. Try to execute the program with the following command:

`sudo python ch04_05.py`

You should see the ball moving from left to right and back again on two 8 x 8 LED dot matrix display modules, as shown in the following screenshot:

You can see this demo on YouTube at `http://youtu.be/F8kDpTz5Wjw`.

Summary

We have used an 8 x 8 LED dot matrix display module on Raspberry Pi. The module uses IC MAX7219 as the driver to control the display of LEDs. We also built some programs to get more practices to use the 8 x 8 LED dot matrix display module.

In the next chapter, you will learn to build a light traffic controller by using Raspberry Pi. We will start with designing a light traffic controller and then implementing it.

5
Building Your Own Traffic Light Controller

A traffic light controller is a signaling device positioned at road intersections and used to control road traffic. In this chapter, we will build a traffic light controller using Raspberry Pi.

You will learn the following topics in this chapter:

- Introducing a traffic light controller
- Designing a traffic light controller
- Controlling AC/DC lamps using channel relay modules
- Expanding Raspberry Pi GPIO
- Building a traffic light controller
- Cascading traffic light controllers

Introducing a traffic light controller

You can find traffic light controller devices at road intersections. They're used to manage vehicle movement on the road. Every traffic light consists of three lamps — red, yellow, and green. These colors have the following meaning:

- **Red**: Drivers must stop their vehicle
- **Yellow**: Drivers should prepare to start to drive or start to stop
- **Green**: Drivers must drive their vehicle

A sample traffic light can be seen in the following figure:

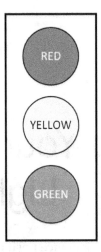

These traffic lights are usually placed at the corner of a road intersection, as shown in the following diagram. You can see them on your left- or right-hand side. Sometimes, they're shown over the top of your vehicle:

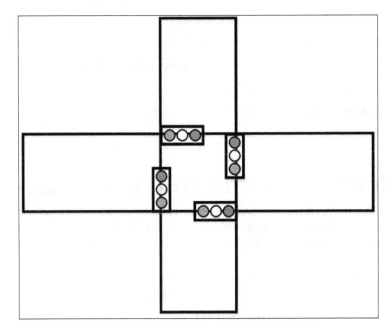

In general, there can be two, three, four or *n* road intersections. We know that a traffic light needs three lamps, so to implement *n* road intersections, you need at least *3n* lamps. You may need walking and *do not work* lamps. Some traffic road intersections can be seen in the following figure:

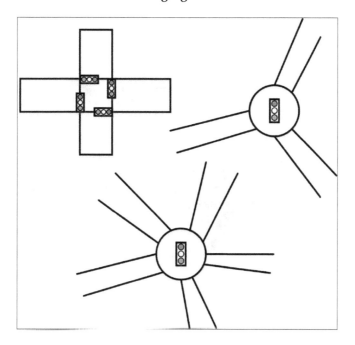

In this chapter, I will show you how to build a traffic light controller with four road intersections. In addition, I will share how to cascade our traffic light controller for several road intersections.

Designing a traffic light controller

To design a traffic light controller, you should identify what kind of road intersection model and connecting module among the lamps you want to build. For instance, if you want to build a traffic light controller for a four-road intersection, you need 12 lamps. This model needs at least 12 pins on Raspberry Pi GPIO.

In the real implementation process, lamps in a traffic light controller use AC as a power source, so you can't connect them to your Raspberry Pi board. It can be addressed by using a channel relay. A sample of a channel relay form can be seen in the following figure:

Some channel relay modules provide wireless links, such as radio, WiFi and XBee, which can be used by **Microcontrollers (MCUs)** to control these modules, so you don't need cables to connect lamps to MCU.

Controlling AC/DC lamps using channel relay modules

A channel relay is a large mechanical switch. This switch is toggled on or off by energizing a coil. Wiring between the I/O control and the relay output does not connect with each other, so the MCU, which controls the I/O relay, is safe. For further information about how to use a relay, read the article available at http://www.circuitstoday.com/working-of-relays.

You can buy a channel relay module from your local electronics or online stores. The following are the online stores to get this stuff:

- Sainsmart, http://www.sainsmart.com/arduino/arduino-components/relays.html

- Sparkfun, https://www.sparkfun.com/products/11042

- DFRobot, http://www.dfrobot.com/index.php?route=product/product&product_id=992

- Amazon, http://www.amazon.com/

- SunFounder, http://www.sunfounder.com/

- LinkSprite, http://store.linksprite.com/

If you note a channel relay module, you should see some of the output pins, such as *COM, N/A, NO*, and *NC*, on the relay module body. These pin names stand for the following:

- **COM(IN)**: This is an input positive wire from the appliance

- **N/A**: This indicates no connection

- **NO**: This is normally open, which means that when the relay is on (a digital high *1* is received from an embedded board), the device is on

- **NC**: This is normally closed, which means that when the relay is off (a digital low *0* is received from an embedded board), the device is on

You can connect the electrical device to the relay module either via **NO** and **COM** or **COM** and **NIC**. The wiring is depicted in the following figure:

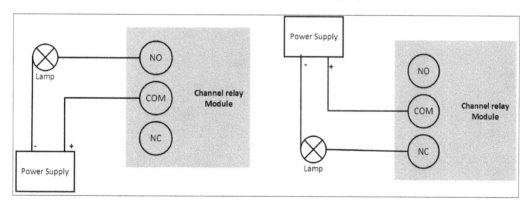

For the demo purpose, we will use a channel relay with Raspberry Pi. The following is our wiring for the demo:

- The relay input pin is connected to *GPIO18* on a Raspberry Pi board
- The relay *VCC* pin is connected to *VCC* +5 V Raspberry Pi
- The relay *GND* pin is connected to *GND* Raspberry Pi
- The relay *NC* pin is connected to the −V lamp
- The relay *COM* pin is connected to the +V lamp

The following is the wiring of this demo:

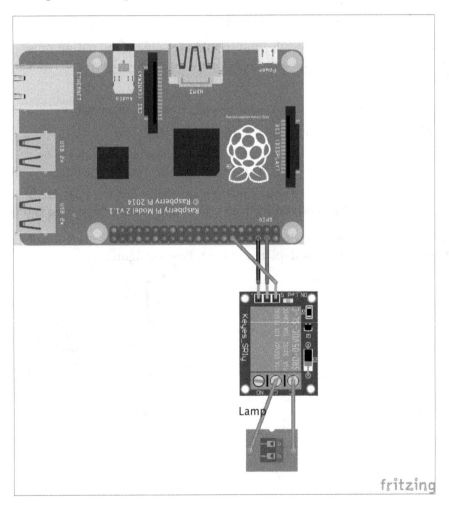

A sample of the wiring implementation is shown in following figure:

Now we start to write a program. Because we connect our lamp to the *NC* pin, it means we can turn on the lamp by sending a *high* value to the channel relay module. We will develop a simple app for blinking lamps.

In our program, we use the WiringPi library to access Raspberry Pi GPIO. Create a file named ch05_01.py and write the following completed code:

```
# ch05_01.py

import wiringpi2 as wiringpi
import time

# initialize
wiringpi.wiringPiSetup()

# define GPIO mode
GPIO18 = 1
LOW = 0
```

```
HIGH = 1
OUTPUT = 1
wiringpi.pinMode(GPIO18, OUTPUT)


# turn on LED sequentially
try:
    while 1:
        print("turn on Lamp")
        wiringpi.digitalWrite(GPIO18, HIGH)
        time.sleep(2)
        print("turn off Lamp")
        wiringpi.digitalWrite(GPIO18, LOW)
        time.sleep(2)

except KeyboardInterrupt:
    wiringpi.digitalWrite(GPIO18, LOW)

print("done")
```

Here is the explanation:

- Initialize the WiringPi library by calling `wiringPiSetup()`
- Define *GPIO18* as an output, which is used for a channel relay input
- Do a looping using the `while` syntax
- In the looping program, turn on the lamp by sending the *high* value via `digitalWrite()`
- To turn off the lamp, send the *low* value to the relay module via `digitalWrite()`
- Set the delay of about *2* seconds between turning on and turning off by calling `time.sleep(2)`; you may change the delay time to investigate the program

Save this file. You can run this program by typing the following command:

```
sudo python ch05_01.py
```

If successful, you should see the red light blinking on your circuit. You should see the program output on the terminal too, as shown in following image:

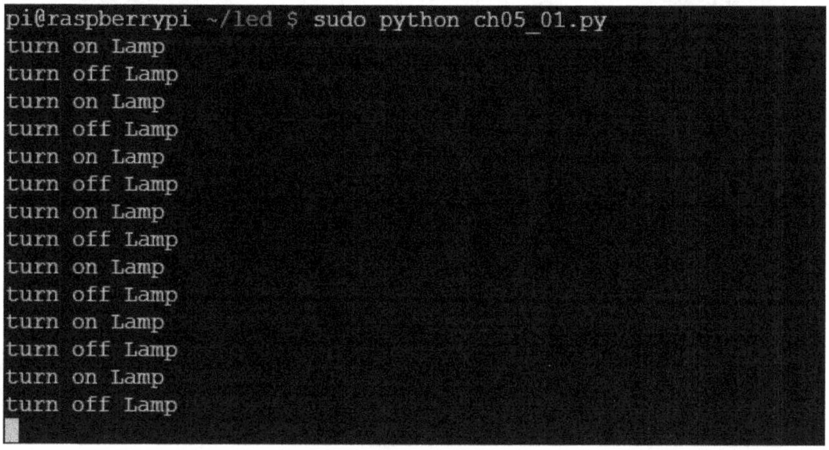

```
pi@raspberrypi ~/led $ sudo python ch05_01.py
turn on Lamp
turn off Lamp
turn on Lamp
turn off Lamp
turn on Lamp
turn off Lamp
turn on Lamp
turn off Lamp
turn on Lamp
turn off Lamp
turn on Lamp
turn off Lamp
turn on Lamp
turn off Lamp
```

Expanding Raspberry Pi GPIO

Let's consider that you want to build a five-road intersection model. This means that you need at least 15 pins on Raspberry Pi GPIO. As you know, Raspberry Pi GPIO has limited pins, so we need to expand Raspberry Pi GPIO.

There are many approaches to expand Raspberry Pi 2. In *Chapter 2*, *Make Your Own Countdown Timer*, and *Chapter 3*, *Make Your Own Digital Clock Display*, we already learned how to expand Raspberry Pi GPIO via the shift register method. Now, you will see how to expand Raspberry Pi GPIO using another approach. Let's introduce the IC MCP23017. It's a 16-bit **input/output (I/O)** port expander with interrupt output and able to be cascaded for up to eight devices on one bus. The MCP23017 uses I2C for communication. Comparing with SPI, I2C uses a bus system with bidirectional data on the SDA line. Otherwise, SPI is a point-to-point connection with data in and data out on separate lines, MOSI and MISO. To communicate devices through I2C, you need to specify a I2C address.

For further information about the IC MCP23017, you can read the datasheet document at http://www.microchip.com/wwwproducts/Devices.aspx?product=MCP23017. This chip is cheap, and you can get this stuff easily from your local electronics or online store. A sample of the scheme of the IC MCP23017 can be seen in the following figure:

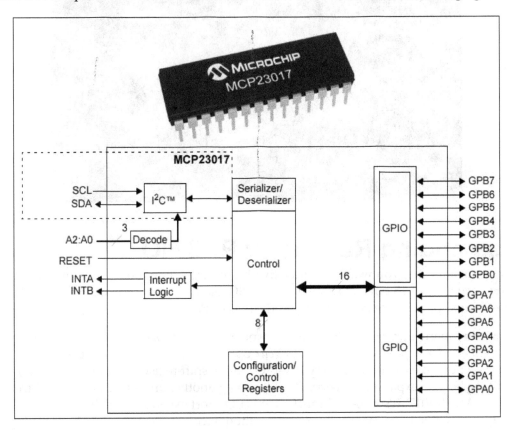

You can control I/O on the MCP23017 via I2C on Raspberry Pi. We already learned how to work with I2C on Raspberry Pi in *Chapter 3, Make Your Own Digital Clock Display*. To write a program based on I2C, we can use the python-smbus module. We are going to use the same approach to access the IC MCP23017.

To understand the working of the IC MCP23017, we will build a simple program to control three LEDs, which are connected to this chip.

The following hardware is needed:

- A Raspberry Pi board
- An IC MCP23017
- Three LEDs
- Cables

Based on the datasheet of the IC MCP23017, you can see this DIP model in the following diagram:

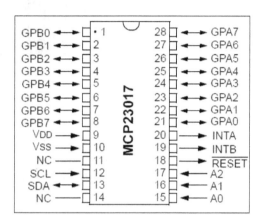

Since the IC MCP23017 has 16-bit I/O pins, you can see the first 8-bit pins located on *GPA0* to *GPA7* and the second 8-bit pins held by *GPB0* to *GPB7*. In this demo, we use only three pins on *GPA0*, *GPA1*, and *GPA2*.

To implement our wiring, you connect the parts as follows:

- *SCL* (pin 12) of the MCP23017 is connected to *GPIO3* (SCL) Raspberry Pi
- *SDA* (pin 13) of the MCP23017 is connected to *GPIO2* (SDA) Raspberry Pi
- *VDD* (pin 9) of the MCP23017 is connected to *VCC* +3.3 V Raspberry Pi
- *VSS* (pin 10) of the MCP23017 is connected to *GND* Raspberry Pi
- *RESET* (pin 18) of the MCP23017 is connected to *VCC* +3.3 V Raspberry Pi
- *GPA0* (pin 21) of the MCP23017 is connected to LED 1
- *GPA1* (pin 22) of the MCP23017 is connected to LED 2
- *GPA2* (pin 23) of the MCP23017 is connected to LED 3
- *A0* (pin 15), *A1* (pin 16), and *A2* (pin 17) are connected to *VCC* +3.3 V Raspberry Pi

The wiring of this demo is shown in the following figure:

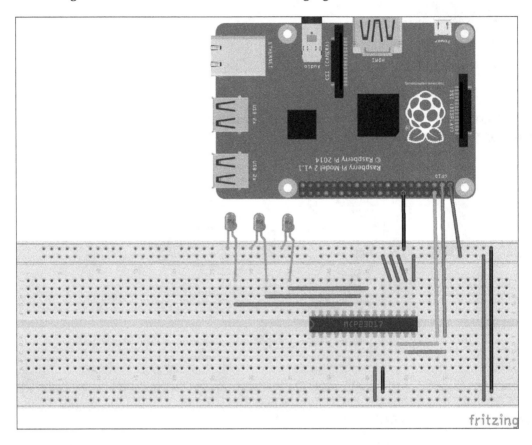

A sample of my wiring implementation can be seen in the following figure:

After completing the wiring, you can plug the DC adapter into Raspberry Pi to power up the board. To verify that our wiring is correct, you can use a i2cdetect tool, a part of I2C tools. Please read *Chapter 3*, *Make Your Own Digital Clock Display* to review Raspberry Pi I2C.

Type the following command:

```
sudo i2cdetect -y 1
```

This works for Raspberry Pi 2 and revision 2. You can check it by typing the following command if you don't see anything:

```
sudo i2cdetect -y 0
```

Because *A0*, *A1*, and *A2* pins of the IC MCP23017 are to be set to *high*, the chip will be recognized on address `0x27`. You should see a sample output in the following figure:

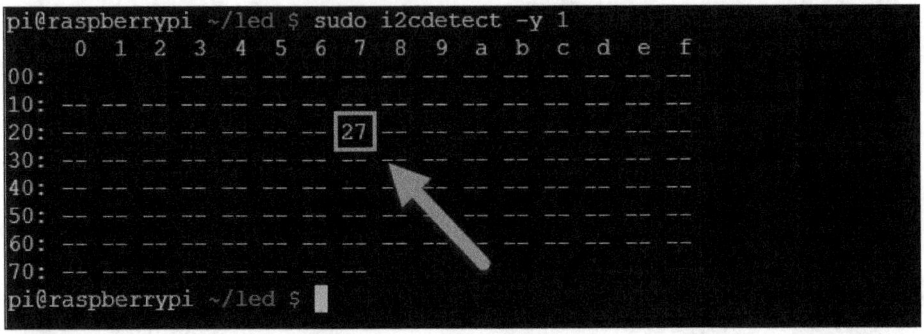

From the preceding figure, the IC MCP23017 was recognized on I2C bus *1*, so you pass the value *1* as the parameter on python-smbus.

Now you're ready to write a program. For testing, we will build a program for LED sequential lights, which uses three LEDs. Based on the IC MCP23017 datasheet, we can work with output port *A* with address `0x00` and port *B* with `0x01`. To define the output mode on pins, we set `0x14` into the register port.

Let's start writing the program. Create a file, named `ch05_02.py`, and write the following complete code:

```
# ch05_02.py

import smbus
import time

bus = smbus.SMBus(1) # Pi 2

MCP32017 = 0x27 # address (A0-A2).You can change it.
IODIRA = 0x00 # Pin A direction register
IODIRB = 0x01 # Pin B direction register
OUTPUT  = 0x14 # Register for outputs
```

```
# all bits of IODIRA register to 0
bus.write_byte_data(MCP32017,IODIRA,0x00)

# Set output all 7 output bits to 0
bus.write_byte_data(MCP32017,OUTPUT,0)

# turn on LED sequentially
try:
    while 1:
        print("LED 1")
        bus.write_byte_data(MCP32017,OUTPUT,0b00000001)
        time.sleep(2)
        print("LED 2")
        bus.write_byte_data(MCP32017,OUTPUT,0b00000010)
        time.sleep(2)
        print("LED 3")
        bus.write_byte_data(MCP32017,OUTPUT,0b00000100)
        time.sleep(2)

except KeyboardInterrupt:
    bus.write_byte_data(MCP32017,OUTPUT,0)

print("done")
```

Here is the explanation:

- Initialize I2C via SMBus for I2C1. You can check I2C1 or I2C0 for your device using the i2cdetect tool
- Set I/O port *A* of the IC MCP23017 to 0
- Set output of I/O port *A* to 0
- Turn on LED 1 by sending 0b00000001 to I/O port *A* using the write_byte_data() function
- Turn on LED 2 by sending 0b00000010 to I/O port *A* using the write_byte_data() function
- Turn on LED 3 by sending 0b00000100 to I/O port *A* using the write_byte_data() function

Now you can execute this program. Type the following command:

```
sudo python ch05_02.py
```

You should see the LED sequential light. I have uploaded this running demo on YouTube. You can see it at `http://youtube/aXckEjPmEWA`. The program displays the output as shown in the following figure:

```
pi@raspberrypi ~/led $ sudo python ch05_02.py
LED 1
LED 2
LED 3
LED 1
LED 2
LED 3
LED 1
LED 2
LED 3
LED 1
LED 2
LED 3
LED 1
```

Building a traffic light controller

After having understood about a traffic light controller and learned how to use a channel relay and how to expand Raspberry Pi GPIO, you are ready to build a traffic light controller.

For testing, we will build a traffic light controller for four road intersections with the following scenario:

- First, we set all intersections showing the red lamp
- To execute traffic light 1, we turn on the yellow lamp and then turn on the green lamp
- After this, we turn on the red lamp on traffic light 1
- Repeat these steps for traffic lights 2, 3, and 4

The following hardware is needed:

- A Raspberry Pi board
- Twelve lamps with four red lamps, four yellow lamps, and four green lamps
- A 4 x 3-channel relay module
- An IC MCP23017
- Cables

In this case, you can ignore channel relay modules if you use a +3 V/+5 V LED, so LEDs can be connected to the IC MCP23017 pins directly. To simplify this demo, we use DC LEDs and don't need many-channel relay modules.

To implement our wiring, you connect all the parts as follows:

- *SCL* (pin 12) of the MCP23017 is connected to *GPIO3* (SCL) Raspberry Pi
- *SDA* (pin 13) of the MCP23017 is connected to *GPIO2* (SDA) Raspberry Pi
- *VDD* (pin 9) of the MCP23017 is connected to *VCC* +3.3 V Raspberry Pi
- *VSS* (pin 10) of the MCP23017 is connected to *GND* Raspberry Pi
- *RESET* (pin 18) of the MCP23017 is connected to *VCC* +3.3 V Raspberry Pi
- *A0* (pin 15), *A1* (pin 16), and *A2* (pin 17) are connected to *VCC* +3.3 V Raspberry Pi

Since we implement four intersections, we define the wiring of traffic lights as follows:

- Intersection−1
    - *GPA0* (pin 21) of the MCP23017 is connected to the red LED
    - *GPA1* (pin 22) of the MCP23017 is connected to the yellow LED
    - *GPA2* (pin 23) of the MCP23017 is connected to the green LED

- Intersection−2
    - *GPA3* (pin 24) of the MCP23017 is connected to the red LED
    - *GPA4* (pin 25) of the MCP23017 is connected to the yellow LED
    - *GPA5* (pin 26) of the MCP23017 is connected to the green LED

- Intersection−3
    - *GPA6* (pin 27) of the MCP23017 is connected to the red LED
    - *GPA7* (pin 28) of the MCP23017 is connected to the yellow LED
    - *GPB0* (pin 1) of the MCP23017 is connected to the green LED

- Intersection−4
    - *GPB1* (pin 2) of the MCP23017 is connected to the red LED
    - *GPB2* (pin 3) of the MCP23017 is connected to the yellow LED
    - *GPB3* (pin 4) of the MCP23017 is connected to the green LED

You can see this wiring in the following figure:

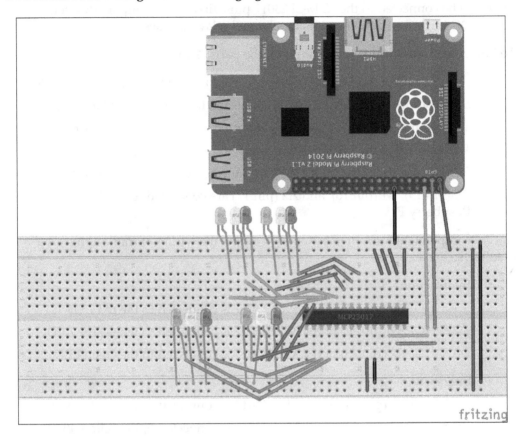

The following is the wiring implementation:

The next step is to build a program for a traffic light controller. The idea is similar as the previous section.

To turn on/off a specific LED, we should send 16-bit data. The following is a table of bit message for the IC MCP23017:

GPBx								GPAx							
15	14	13	12	11	10	9	8	7	6	5	4	3	2	1	0
xxx				IR 4			IR 3			IR 2			IR 1		
x	x	x	x	G	Y	R	G	Y	R	G	Y	R	G	Y	R

Note the following:

- **IR is intersection road**
- **R is red**
- **Y is yellow**
- **G is green**

For example, we want to turn on all the red LEDs, so we can define the following bits:

GPBx								GPAx							
15	14	13	12	11	10	9	8	7	6	5	4	3	2	1	0
xxx				IR 4			IR 3			IR 2			IR 1		
x	x	x	x	G	Y	R	G	Y	R	G	Y	R	G	Y	R
0	0	0	0	0	0	1	0	0	1	0	0	1	0	0	1

For this table, we send 01001001 to *GPA* port from the IC MCP23017 and 00000010 to *GPB* port. Based on the IC MCP23017 datasheet, the address of port *A* and port *B* are 0x14 and 0x15, respectively.

First, create a file named ch05_03.py, and write the complete code as follows:

```
# ch05_03.py

import smbus
import time

bus = smbus.SMBus(1) # Pi 2

MCP32017 = 0x27 # address (A0-A2).You can change it.
IODIRA = 0x00 # Pin A direction register
IODIRB = 0x01 # Pin B direction register
```

```
OUTPUTA  = 0x14 # Register for output A
OUTPUTB  = 0x15 # Register for output B

def turn_off_all():
    bus.write_byte_data(MCP32017,OUTPUTA,0)
    bus.write_byte_data(MCP32017,OUTPUTB,0)

def turn_on_red_all():
    bus.write_byte_data(MCP32017,OUTPUTA,0b01001001)
    bus.write_byte_data(MCP32017,OUTPUTB,0b00000010)

def go_traffic(intersection):
    if intersection==1:
        print(">>>yellow")
        bus.write_byte_data(MCP32017,OUTPUTA,0b01001010)
        bus.write_byte_data(MCP32017,OUTPUTB,0b00000010)
        time.sleep(2)
        print(">>>green")
        bus.write_byte_data(MCP32017,OUTPUTA,0b01001100)
        bus.write_byte_data(MCP32017,OUTPUTB,0b00000010)
        time.sleep(3)

    if intersection==2:
        print(">>>yellow")
        bus.write_byte_data(MCP32017,OUTPUTA,0b01010001)
        bus.write_byte_data(MCP32017,OUTPUTB,0b00000010)
        time.sleep(2)
        print(">>>green")
        bus.write_byte_data(MCP32017,OUTPUTA,0b01100001)
        bus.write_byte_data(MCP32017,OUTPUTB,0b00000010)
        time.sleep(3)

    if intersection==3:
        print(">>>yellow")
        bus.write_byte_data(MCP32017,OUTPUTA,0b10001001)
        bus.write_byte_data(MCP32017,OUTPUTB,0b00000010)
        time.sleep(2)
        print(">>>green")
        bus.write_byte_data(MCP32017,OUTPUTA,0b00001001)
        bus.write_byte_data(MCP32017,OUTPUTB,0b00000011)
        time.sleep(3)
```

```
        if intersection==4:
            print(">>>yellow")
            bus.write_byte_data(MCP32017,OUTPUTA,0b01001001)
            bus.write_byte_data(MCP32017,OUTPUTB,0b00000100)
            time.sleep(2)
            print(">>>green")
            bus.write_byte_data(MCP32017,OUTPUTA,0b01001001)
            bus.write_byte_data(MCP32017,OUTPUTB,0b00001000)
            time.sleep(3)

    # all bits of registers to 0
    bus.write_byte_data(MCP32017,IODIRA,0x00)
    bus.write_byte_data(MCP32017,IODIRB,0x00)

    turn_off_all()
    turn_on_red_all()

    try:
        while 1:
            print("road 1")
            go_traffic(1)
            turn_off_all()
            print("road 2")
            go_traffic(2)
            turn_off_all()
            print("road 3")
            go_traffic(3)
            turn_off_all()
            print("road 4")
            go_traffic(4)
            turn_off_all()

    except KeyboardInterrupt:
        turn_off_all()

    print("done")
```

Here is the explanation:

- Initialize I2C via SMBus for I2C1.
- Set I/O port *A* to 0.
- Set the output of I/O port *A* and *B* to 0 for initialization.

- Define `turn_off_all()` to turn off all LEDs.

- Define `turn_on_red_all()` to turn on red LEDs.

- Define `go_traffic()` function to activate which traffic light runs.

- To turn on yellow and green LEDs, you can send `0b01001010` and `0b01001100`. Please read the explanation given in the previous paragraph.

- Repeat the same steps for road intersections 2, 3, and 4.

If finished, you can run the program by typing the following command:

```
sudo python ch05_03.py
```

You should see the program output on the terminal. I have already uploaded a running demo of this app. You can see it on YouTube, http://youtu.be/jbKVAIwggUE.

```
pi@raspberrypi ~/led $ sudo python ch05_03.py
road 1
>>>yellow
>>>green
road 2
>>>yellow
>>>green
road 3
>>>yellow
>>>green
road 4
>>>yellow
>>>green
road 1
```

Cascading traffic light controllers

You may want to control many traffic light controllers via one board, that is, Raspberry Pi 2. It's possible. You just expand Raspberry Pi GPIO according to your needs. In the previous section, we already learned how to expand Raspberry Pi GPIO using the IC MCP23017. How to work with more than one IC MCP23017?

You can implement it with the following configuration:

- You can connect the *SCL* and *SDA* pins to the same pin for I2C

- Set the module address (*A0*, *A1*, and *A2*) with different address, for instance, IC1 `000` and IC2 `111`

Now, you can connect the lamps to the IC MCP23017 output pins as usual. The following is a sample of the wiring implementation:

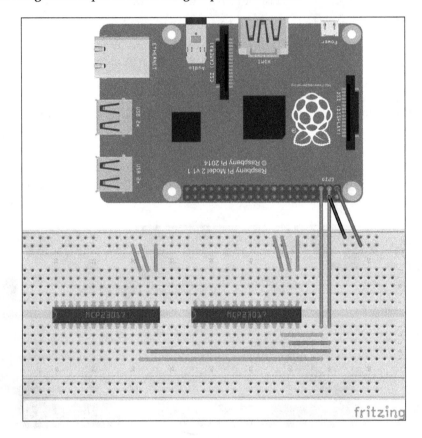

From the preceding figure, you can do construct the following wiring:

- All IC MCP23017 *SDA* pins are connected to Raspberry Pi *SDA*
- All IC MCP23017 *SCL* pins are connected to Raspberry Pi *SCL*
- All IC MCP23017 *VCC* pins are connected to Raspberry Pi +5 V
- All IC MCP23017 *GND* pins are connected to Raspberry Pi *GND*

The following is the wiring implementation:

The next is to write a program. You can write a program using I2C as usual. Make sure that each IC MCP23017 already sets its I2C address through *A0*, *A1*, and *A2* pins.

Summary

We already learned about a traffic light controller. The chapter introduced a road intersection module at the start. A channel relay module is introduced in order to work with AC or high-voltage lamps. We also learned how to expand our Raspberry Pi GPIO. After this, we built a traffic light controller for four road intersections. In the last section, we tried to cascade our traffic controller by connecting several IC MCP23017.

In the next chapter, we will learn to control sensor or actuator devices via Bluetooth from a Raspberry Pi board.

6
Building Your Own Light Controller-based Bluetooth

Bluetooth is a communication technology that enables devices to communicate with others. In this chapter, we will build a light controller-based Bluetooth on a Raspberry Pi board. We can control our LEDs, lamps, or other devices from any device with a supporting Bluetooth stack.

You will learn the following topics in this chapter:

- Introducing Bluetooth
- Working with Bluetooth using Raspberry Pi
- Introducing iBeacon
- Bluetooth programming on Android
- Building a remote light controller-based Bluetooth

Introducing Bluetooth

Bluetooth is a communication technology that enables devices to communicate with other devices. It's a part of **wireless personal area network (WPAN)** technology. In real life, we can see that some electronic devices can be controlled via Bluetooth network, for instance, listening to music using Bluetooth earphones, transferring a file, and gathering sensing data.

Currently, the Bluetooth specification is managed by **Bluetooth Special Interest Group (SIG)**. They developed Bluetooth standards and specifications. Bluetooth 4.3 was released in December 2014. Since Bluetooth 4.x released, this standard is named as **Bluetooth Low Energy (BLE)**. Sometimes, it's called **Bluetooth smart technology**.

OS X, Linux, and Windows 8.x / 10, natively support BLE and mobile OS, including iOS, Android, Windows phone, and BlackBerry. If your desktop OS doesn't support BLE, you can install a BLE driver based on the hardware stack.

Not all Bluetooth devices support BLE. You can verify this from the device information, such as device manager or system information. For instance, in OS X, you should see it on system information, shown in **Hardware - Bluetooth**. It displays **Bluetooth Low Energy Supported: Yes**:

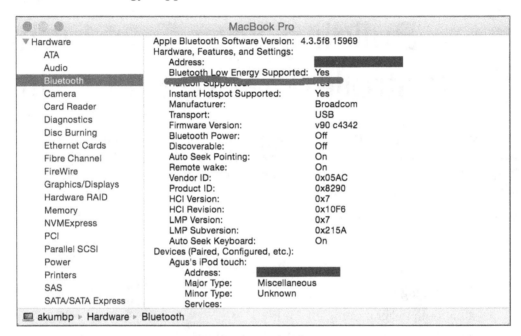

Working with Bluetooth using Raspberry Pi

Raspberry Pi doesn't come with a Bluetooth module in its board, so if you want to work with Bluetooth stacks, you should attach a Bluetooth module. The easier approach to attach a Bluetooth module into a Raspberry Pi board is to use Bluetooth USBs. There are many Bluetooth USB devices.

However, some Bluetooth USB devices are only compatible with Raspberry Pi. The following is a list of the tested Bluetooth USBs:

- Bluetooth 4.0 USB Module (v2.1 Back-Compatible), http://www.adafruit.com/products/1327

- JBtek, http://www.amazon.com/JBtek-Raspberry-Bluetooth-4-0-adapter/dp/B00L08NCPQ/

- Black Bluetooth CSR 4.0, http://www.amazon.com/Black-Bluetooth-Dongle-Adapter-Raspberry/dp/B010LOY438/

- Pluggable USB Bluetooth 4, http://www.amazon.com/Plugable-Bluetooth-Adapter-Raspberry-Compatible/dp/B009ZIILLI/

- USB BLE Link, http://www.dfrobot.com/index.php?route=product/product&product_id=1220

 For further information about Bluetooth USBs for Raspberry Pi, refer to http://elinux.org/RPi_USB_Bluetooth_adapters.

Some of these Bluetooth USBs are shown in the following image:

In addition, you can use a Bluetooth module that is attached to a Raspberry Pi board via SPI, I2C, or UART. The following is a list of Bluetooth module samples:

- Bluetooth products from Tinysine, `http://www.tinyosshop.com/index.php?route=product/category&path=65_110`

- A BLE link, `http://www.dfrobot.com/index.php?route=product/product&product_id=1073&search=ble&description=true#.VbOyN3gkKfQ`

- DFRobot Bluetooth v3, `http://www.dfrobot.com/index.php?route=product/product&product_id=360#.VbO67XgkKfQ`

In the next section, we're going to set up and test Bluetooth USBs on the Raspberry Pi board.

Setting up a Bluetooth USB

In this section, we try to set up our Bluetooth USB with Raspberry Pi. To work with a Bluetooth stack, we need a Bluetooth library. We use the BlueZ library (`http://www.bluez.org`). First, you need to install all the required libraries for BlueZ. Type the following commands:

```
$ sudo apt-get update
$ sudo apt-get install libdbus-1-dev libdbus-glib-1-dev libglib2.0-dev libical-dev libreadline-dev libudev-dev libusb-dev make
```

After that, you download the BlueZ library. For instance, we use BlueZ 5.32. Then, download and extract it using the following commands:

```
$ wget https://www.kernel.org/pub/linux/bluetooth/bluez-5.32.tar.xz
$ tar xvf bluez-5.32.tar.xz
```

If finished, you can install the following library:

```
$ cd bluez-5.32
$ ./configure --disable-systemd
$ make
$ sudo make install
```

Now you can attach the Bluetooth USB to the Raspberry Pi board. Then, you can verify it using `lsusb`:

```
$ lsusb
```

You should get the Bluetooth USB with product ID information. For instance, we will use Bluetooth 4.0 USB from CSR. It shows ID `0a12`, so type this command to get Bluetooth device information:

```
$ sudo lsusb -v -d 0a12:
```

The information obtained is as shown in the following screenshot:

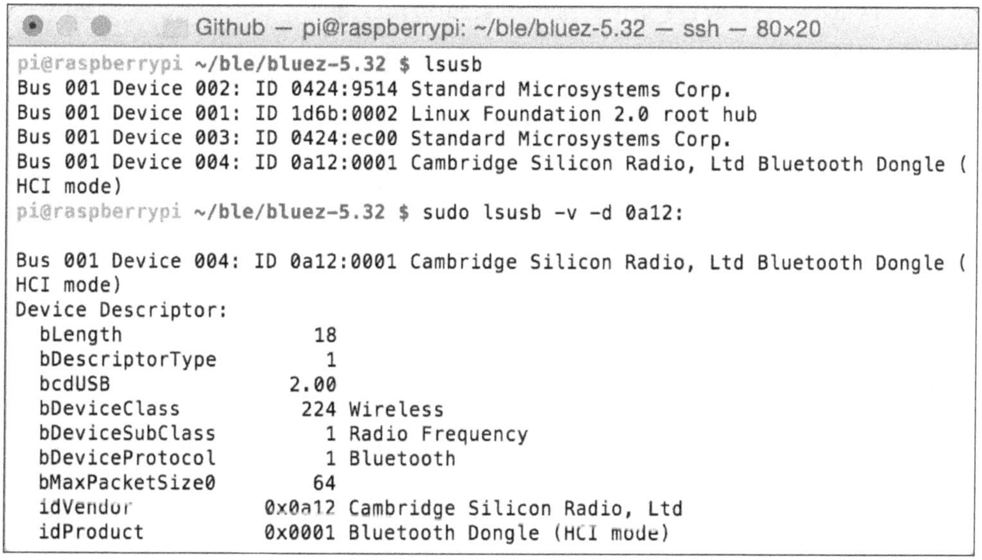

```
Github — pi@raspberrypi: ~/ble/bluez-5.32 — ssh — 80×20
pi@raspberrypi ~/ble/bluez-5.32 $ lsusb
Bus 001 Device 002: ID 0424:9514 Standard Microsystems Corp.
Bus 001 Device 001: ID 1d6b:0002 Linux Foundation 2.0 root hub
Bus 001 Device 003: ID 0424:ec00 Standard Microsystems Corp.
Bus 001 Device 004: ID 0a12:0001 Cambridge Silicon Radio, Ltd Bluetooth Dongle (
HCI mode)
pi@raspberrypi ~/ble/bluez-5.32 $ sudo lsusb -v -d 0a12:

Bus 001 Device 004: ID 0a12:0001 Cambridge Silicon Radio, Ltd Bluetooth Dongle (
HCI mode)
Device Descriptor:
  bLength                18
  bDescriptorType         1
  bcdUSB               2.00
  bDeviceClass          224 Wireless
  bDeviceSubClass         1 Radio Frequency
  bDeviceProtocol         1 Bluetooth
  bMaxPacketSize0        64
  idVendor           0x0a12 Cambridge Silicon Radio, Ltd
  idProduct          0x0001 Bluetooth Dongle (HCI mode)
```

Turning on/off Bluetooth

To check whether the Bluetooth USB is up or not, you can use the `hciconfig` command. Type the following command:

```
$ hciconfig
```

You should see that the Bluetooth device information includes the address and device state—**UP** or **DOWN**.

To turn on the Bluetooth USB, you can pass up a parameter on **hciconfig**. For instance, the Bluetooth USB device is recognized as `hci0`:

```
$ sudo hciconfig hci0 up
```

In the following screenshot, you can see a sample output of executing command:

```
●  ●  ●          Github — pi@raspberrypi: ~/ble/bluez-5.32 — ssh — 80×20
pi@raspberrypi ~/ble/bluez-5.32 $ hciconfig
hci0:   Type: BR/EDR  Bus: USB
        BD Address: 00:1A:7D:DA:71:13  ACL MTU: 310:10  SCO MTU: 64:8
        DOWN
        RX bytes:564 acl:0 sco:0 events:29 errors:0
        TX bytes:358 acl:0 sco:0 commands:29 errors:0

pi@raspberrypi ~/ble/bluez-5.32 $ sudo hciconfig hci0 up
pi@raspberrypi ~/ble/bluez-5.32 $ hciconfig
hci0:   Type: BR/EDR  Bus: USB
        BD Address: 00:1A:7D:DA:71:13  ACL MTU: 310:10  SCO MTU: 64:8
        UP RUNNING
        RX bytes:1128 acl:0 sco:0 events:58 errors:0
        TX bytes:716 acl:0 sco:0 commands:58 errors:0

pi@raspberrypi ~/ble/bluez-5.32 $ █
```

If you want to turn off your Bluetooth USB, you pass the down parameter on the hciconfig tool:

```
$ sudo hciconfig hci0 down
```

In this state, the Bluetooth device doesn't receive or send any message.

Enabling discoverable

By default, our Bluetooth USB cannot be searched by other Bluetooth devices. You can enable discoverable on the Bluetooth USB by passing the piscan parameter on hciconfig as follows:

```
$ sudo hciconfig hci0 piscan
```

When done, your Bluetooth USB can be detected on a Bluetooth app, for instance, the Bluetooth from Raspberry Pi is detected by OS X as follows:

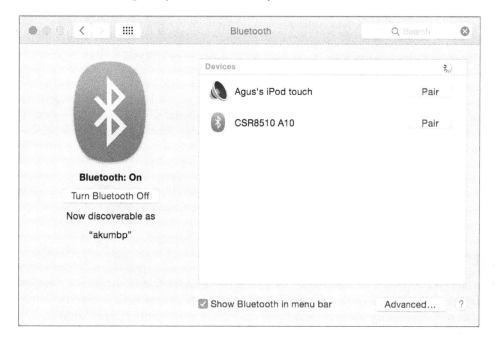

Scanning for Bluetooth Devices

You also can find other Bluetooth devices using hcitool by passing the scan parameter. Type the following command:

```
$ hcitool scan
```

When done, you should see a list of Bluetooth devices that are running. It displays Bluetooth address and name, as shown in the following screenshot:

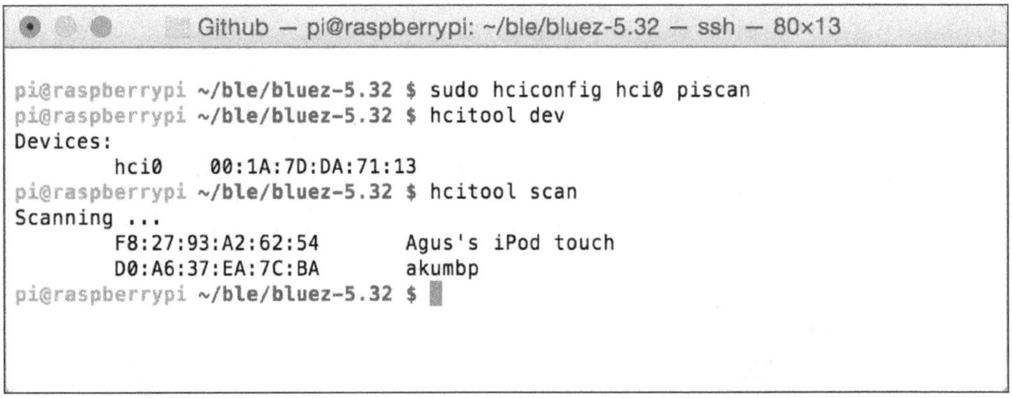

```
● ● ●          Github — pi@raspberrypi: ~/ble/bluez-5.32 — ssh — 80×13

pi@raspberrypi ~/ble/bluez-5.32 $ sudo hciconfig hci0 piscan
pi@raspberrypi ~/ble/bluez-5.32 $ hcitool dev
Devices:
        hci0    00:1A:7D:DA:71:13
pi@raspberrypi ~/ble/bluez-5.32 $ hcitool scan
Scanning ...
        F8:27:93:A2:62:54        Agus's iPod touch
        D0:A6:37:EA:7C:BA        akumbp
pi@raspberrypi ~/ble/bluez-5.32 $ █
```

Introducing iBeacon

iBeacon is a proprietary technology from Apple, which adds additional services to a BLE stack. It usually provides location services on an iBeacon stack. An iBeacon stack consists of **universally unique identifier (UUID)** — major and minor values. How to implement iBeacon on Raspberry Pi? In the previous section, we already set up our Bluetooth on Raspberry Pi.

Now we build iBeacon on the Bluetooth 4 (BLE) stack. Make sure that you have already set up Bluetooth on Raspberry Pi. Please read this in the previous section.

After attaching the Bluetooth 4.0 USB to the Raspberry Pi board, turn on and configure it. Type the following commands:

```
$ sudo hciconfig hci0 up
$ sudo hciconfig hci0 leadv 3
$ sudo hciconfig hci0 noscan
```

We pass the `leadv 3` parameters on `hciconfig` to disable the advertised service connectable. The `noscan` parameter is used to disable our Bluetooth device to do scanning.

The next step is to send an iBeacon packet. To transmit an iBeacon packet, you can use `hcitool` using the following command:

```
sudo hcitool -i hci0 cmd 0x08 0x0008 package_flag vendor_info uuid major
minor power
```

For testing purpose, we use the following parameters:

- `package_flag`: 1E 02 01 1A 1A
- `vendor_info`: FF 4C 00 02 15
- `major`: 00 01
- `minor`: 00 00

To obtain a UUID, you can use Python to generate this UUID. Type the following commands:

```
$ python
>>> import sys,uuid
>>> print(uuid.uuid4().hex)
```

```
pi@raspberrypi ~ $ python
Python 2.7.3 (default, Mar 18 2014, 05:13:23)
[GCC 4.6.3] on linux2
Type "help", "copyright", "credits" or "license" for more information.
>>> import sys,uuid
>>> print(uuid.uuid4().hex)
9d79278addef413cadf6ee51ae5cf29d
>>>
```

When done, you should see that Python has generated a UUID, for instance, `9d79278addef413cadf6ee51ae5cf29d`. It can be represented as `9D 79 27 8A DD EF 41 3C AD F6 EE 51 AE 5C F2 9D`.

Now, let's try to broadcast our iBeacon packet with the following command:

```
sudo hcitool -i hci0 cmd 0x08 0x0008 1E 02 01 1A 1A FF 4C 00 02 15 9D 79
27 8A DD EF 41 3C AD F6 EE 51 AE 5C F2 9D 00 00 01 00 C7 00
```

To read the iBeacon packet, you can use the iBeacon-based app on Android or iOS. For instance, we will use the Bluetooth LE Scanner from the Android Play Store. This tool can also provide the details of the iBeacon packet.

A sample output of BLE scanner tool is shown in following figure:

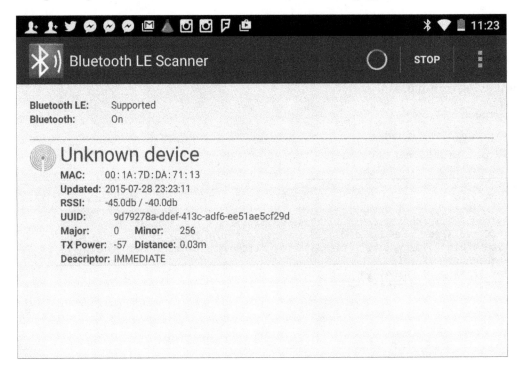

To obtain the details of the Bluetooth device, you can tap the data to see the device information. A sample of the detail information can be seen in the following figure:

Bluetooth programming on Android

An Android platform provides API to access Bluetooth. Not all Android-based smartphones have BLE. There are many tools on Play Store to detect whether Android's Bluetooth is BLE or not.

To work with Bluetooth on Android, we can use the `android.bluetooth` package (`http://developer.android.com/guide/topics/connectivity/bluetooth.html`).

For testing, we build an Android app that retrieves a list of paired Bluetooth devices on an Android device. I use Intellij IDEA, `https://www.jetbrains.com/idea`, but you can also use Android Studio, `http://developer.android.com/sdk/index.html`. Download and install this tool.

Create a new project for Android named `mybluetooth`. First, modify the `AndroidManifest.xml` file to enable Bluetooth features on the Android platform. The following is the `AndroidManifest.xml` file:

```xml
<?xml version="1.0" encoding="utf-8"?>
<manifest xmlns:android="http://schemas.android.com/apk/res/android"
          package="akur.mybluetooth"
          android:versionCode="1"
          android:versionName="1.0">
    <uses-sdk android:minSdkVersion="19"/>
    <uses-permission
    android:name="android.permission.ACCESS_NETWORK_STATE"/>
    <uses-permission
    android:name="android.permission.ACCESS_WIFI_STATE"/>
    <uses-permission android:name="android.permission.BLUETOOTH"/>
    <uses-permission
    android:name="android.permission.BLUETOOTH_ADMIN"/>
    <application android:label="@string/app_name"
    android:icon="@drawable/ic_launcher">
        <activity android:name="MyActivity"
                android:label="@string/app_name">
            <intent-filter>
                <action android:name="android.intent.action.MAIN"/>
                <category
                android:name="android.intent.category.LAUNCHER"/>
            </intent-filter>
        </activity>
    </application>
</manifest>
```

We build an Android UI using TextView, which will render a list of paired Bluetooth devices. Write this script on `main.xml` from the `/res/layout project` folder:

```xml
<?xml version="1.0" encoding="utf-8"?>
<LinearLayout
xmlns:android="http://schemas.android.com/apk/res/android"
            android:orientation="vertical"
            android:layout_width="fill_parent"
            android:layout_height="fill_parent">
    <TextView
            android:id="@+id/tvBlueInfo"
            android:layout_width="wrap_content"
            android:layout_height="wrap_content" />
</LinearLayout>
```

Create a new class named `BlueConnection` to retrieve information from the Bluetooth device. Write the following code into the `BlueConnection.java` file:

```java
package akur.mybluetooth;

import android.bluetooth.BluetoothAdapter;

public class BlueConnection {
  private static boolean state = false;

  public static boolean getBlueTooth() {

    BluetoothAdapter bluetooth =
    BluetoothAdapter.getDefaultAdapter();
    if (!bluetooth.isEnabled()) {
      System.out.println("Bluetooth is Disable...");
      state = true;
    } else if (bluetooth.isEnabled()) {
      String address = bluetooth.getAddress();
      String name = bluetooth.getName();
      System.out.println(name + " : " + address);
      state = false;
    }
  return state;
  }
}
```

The last task is to modify our main program. Modify the `MyActivity.java` file and write the following code:

```java
package akur.mybluetooth;

import java.util.Set;
import android.bluetooth.BluetoothAdapter;
import android.bluetooth.BluetoothDevice;
import android.content.Intent;
import android.widget.TextView;
import android.widget.Toast;

import android.app.Activity;
import android.os.Bundle;

public class MyActivity extends Activity {
  private static final int REQUEST_ENABLE_BT = 12;
  private TextView view;
  private BluetoothAdapter adapter;

  @Override
  public void onCreate(Bundle savedInstanceState) {
    super.onCreate(savedInstanceState);
    setContentView(R.layout.main);

    view = (TextView) findViewById(R.id.tvBlueInfo);
    displayData();

    if (BlueConnection.getBlueTooth()) {
      Intent enableBtIntent = new Intent(
        BluetoothAdapter.ACTION_REQUEST_ENABLE);
        startActivityForResult(enableBtIntent, REQUEST_ENABLE_BT);
    }
  }

  @Override
  protected void onActivityResult(int requestCode, int resultCode,
  Intent data) {
    super.onActivityResult(requestCode, resultCode, data);
    view.setText("");
    displayData();
  }

  private void displayData() {

    adapter = BluetoothAdapter.getDefaultAdapter();
    view.append("\nAdapter: " + adapter.toString() + "\n\nName: "
    + adapter.getName() + "\nAddress: " + adapter.getAddress());
```

```
    if (adapter == null) {
      Toast.makeText(this, "Bluetooth NOT supported. Aborting.",
      Toast.LENGTH_LONG).show();
    }

    view.append("\n\nStarting discovery...");
    adapter.startDiscovery();
    view.append("\nDone with discovery...\n");

    view.append("\nDevices Paired:");
    Set<BluetoothDevice> devices = adapter.getBondedDevices();
    for (BluetoothDevice device : devices) {
      view.append("\nDevice: " + device.getName() + " Add: "
      + device.getAddress());
    }
  }
}
```

Save this project. Compile and build this project into the .apk file. Then, deploy the .apk file into your Android device. I tested and deployed it into a Nexus 7 (generation 2) device.

Now, you can run this program. A sample program output is shown in the following figure:

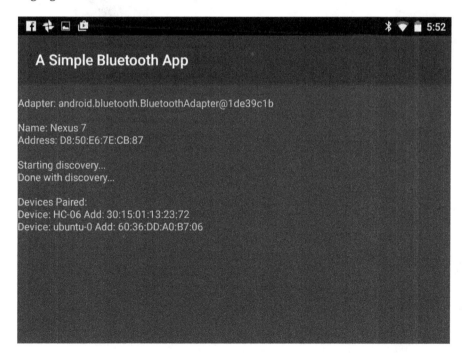

Building a remote light controller-based Bluetooth

In *Chapter 5*, *Building Your Own Traffic Light Controller*, we already developed a traffic light controller. However, we controlled the lamps/LEDs directly from an internal app in Raspberry Pi. In this section, we will build an app that controls actuator or sensor devices on Raspberry Pi remotely via Bluetooth.

For testing, we will use three LEDs as actuator devices, which are controlled from the Android app via the Bluetooth module. We will use the HC-06 Bluetooth serial device, and the price is cheap. This module uses a **Universal Asynchronous Receiver/Transmitter (UART)** to send and receive a Bluetooth packet. You can get this module from eBay, Amazon, or your local electronics store:

Wiring

To build our demo, we need the following hardware:

- A Raspberry Pi board
- An HC-06 Bluetooth serial
- Three LEDs
- Cables

The following is the hardware wiring:

- The HC-06 *TX* is connected to Raspberry Pi *RX*
- The HC-06 *RX* is connected to Raspberry Pi *TX*
- The HC-06 *GND* is connected to Raspberry Pi *GND*
- The HC-06 *VCC* is connected to Raspberry Pi *VCC* +3.3 V
- LED 1 is connected to Raspberry Pi *GPIO17*
- LED 2 is connected to Raspberry Pi *GPIO27*
- LED 3 is connected to Raspberry Pi *GPIO23*
- All LED *GND* pins are connected to Raspberry Pi *GND*

These connections are also shown in the following image:

Building a program for Raspberry Pi

An HC-06 Bluetooth module works with UART, so our Raspberry Pi should be configured to enable UART. By default, UART pins are used as a serial console. Raspberry Pi uses it for debugging. We need to disable this feature to use UART on Raspberry Pi GPIO.

Modify the `/boot/cmdline.txt` file:

```
$ sudo nano /boot/cmdline.txt
```

If you see **console=ttyAMA0, 115200** in this file, please remove it:

A sample file output after modification can be seen in the following figure:

When finished, you must reboot Raspberry Pi.

To build a Python program that uses UART, we can use the `pyserial` library, `https://pypi.python.org/pypi/pyserial`. You can install it via `pip` or `easy_install`:

```
$ pip install pyserial
$ easy_install -U pyserial
```

Now we can write the Python program. The following is our program algorithm:

- Initialize the serial port and GPIO
- Wait for an incoming message from UART
- If UART data = 1, the program will turn on LED 1
- If UART data = 2, the program will turn on LED 2
- If UART data = 3, the program will turn on LED 3
- If UART data = 4, the program will turn off LED 1
- If UART data = 5, the program will turn off LED 2
- If UART data = 6, the program will turn off LED 3

To implement this scenario, write the following complete code:

```
# ch06_01.py

import wiringpi2 as wiringpi
import sys, serial
import time

# initialize
print("initializing...")
wiringpi.wiringPiSetup()

# define GPIO mode
GPIO17 = 0
GPIO27 = 2
GPIO23 = 4
LOW = 0
HIGH = 1
OUTPUT = 1
# define serial port for bluetooth HC-06
port = '/dev/ttyAMA0'
baudrate = 9600

wiringpi.pinMode(GPIO17, OUTPUT)   # LED 1
wiringpi.pinMode(GPIO27, OUTPUT)   # LED 2
wiringpi.pinMode(GPIO23, OUTPUT)   # LED 3
```

```python
def enum(**enums):
    return type('Enum', (), enums)

Status = enum(LED1ON='1', LED2ON='2', LED3ON='3',LED1OFF='4',
LED2OFF='5', LED3OFF='6')

# make all LEDs off
def clear_all():
    wiringpi.digitalWrite(GPIO17, LOW)
    wiringpi.digitalWrite(GPIO27, LOW)
    wiringpi.digitalWrite(GPIO23, LOW)

print("opening serial port")
ser = serial.Serial(port, baudrate, timeout=0)
if ser.isOpen():
    ser.close()
ser.open()
print(ser.isOpen())
print("running now")
# test write
ser.write('9')
try:
    clear_all()
    while 1:
        ret = ''
        #while ser.inWaiting() > 0:
        #ret = ser.read(1)
        ret = ser.readline()

        if ret != '':
            ret = ret.strip("\r\n")
            print "RCV: " + ret
            ser.write("OK")

            if(ret in Status.LED1ON ):
                wiringpi.digitalWrite(GPIO17, HIGH)
            if(ret in Status.LED1OFF ):
                wiringpi.digitalWrite(GPIO17, LOW)
            if(ret in Status.LED2ON ):
                wiringpi.digitalWrite(GPIO27, HIGH)
            if(ret in Status.LED2OFF ):
                wiringpi.digitalWrite(GPIO27, LOW)
            if(ret in Status.LED3ON ):
                wiringpi.digitalWrite(GPIO23, HIGH)
            if(ret in Status.LED3OFF ):
                wiringpi.digitalWrite(GPIO23, LOW)

        time.sleep(1)

except KeyboardInterrupt:
```

```
    clear_all()
    ser.close()

print("done")
```

Save this code into a file named `ch06_01.py`.

Building a Bluetooth app for Android

In this case, we will use the existing Android app from the Play Store. You can use the Bluetooth Terminal app, which is free:

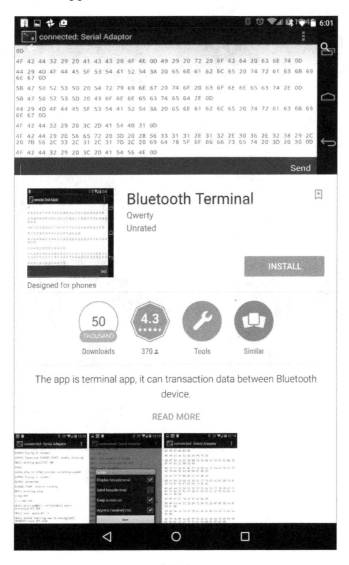

After getting it installed, you can pair HC-06 Bluetooth to Android. By default, the pair key of HC-06 Bluetooth is *1234*.

Testing

The next step is to test our program, ch06_01.py. First, run the Python program on Raspberry Pi:

```
$ sudo python ch06_01.py
```

After that, run Bluetooth Terminal. Select the paired Bluetooth for HC-06. Don't forget to check **Append newline (\r\n)**:

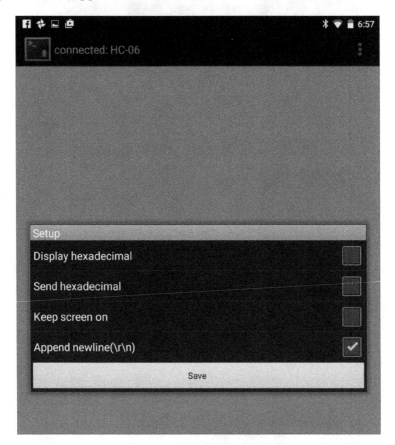

Now, you can try to send message 1, 2, or 3 to turn on LED 1, 2, or 3, respectively. You can send message 4, 5, or 6 to turn off LED 1, 2, or 3, respectively.

A sample hardware output is shown in the following figure:

The program also generated output data in the terminal. You can see it in the following figure:

```
●  ●  ●                codes — pi@raspberrypi: ~/led — ssh — 80×16
pi@raspberrypi ~/led $ sudo python ch06_01.py
initializing...
opening serial port
True
running now
RCV: 1
RCV: 2
RCV: 3
RCV: 4
RCV: 5
RCV: 6
RCV: 2
▉
```

Summary

We already learned how to set up Bluetooth and iBeacon with Raspberry Pi. Furthermore, communication between Raspberry Pi and Android was established via Bluetooth. In the last section, we tried to build a remote light controller which controls LEDs on Raspberry Pi via Bluetooth from Android.

In the next chapter, we will learn how to apply the Internet of things for Raspberry Pi to control LEDs and lamps.

7
Making Your Own Controlled Lamps Through Internet Network

The Internet network connects devices together. Internet coverage is huge. In this chapter, we make our own controlled lamps through Internet network. We can control our LEDs, lamps, or other devices from any device with a supporting Internet network stack.

You will learn the following topics in this chapter:

- Connecting the Raspberry Pi to a network
- Introducing Node.js
- Controlling LEDs and lamps using Node.js
- Building a simple web server using Node.js
- Building RESTful using Node.js
- Controlling LEDs through RESTful
- Building a PhoneGap application for Android
- Connecting PhoneGap Android to Raspberry Pi through RESTful

Connecting the Raspberry Pi to a network

We can obtain information, such as temperature and humidity at a particular location, through the Internet. In daily lives, we use the Internet to surf via a browser. In this section, we will try to connect Raspberry Pi to either a wired or wireless network.

There are many benefits that we can obtain while connecting Raspberry Pi to a network. We can retrieve sensor data or just control actuator devices on Raspberry Pi.

Connecting to a wired network

By default, Raspberry Pi, such as Raspberry Pi 2 model B and Raspberry Pi 1 model B+, has installed Ethernet, so we can connect it to a network via a UTP cable. If a UTP cable is connected to the Internet network, Raspberry Pi will be able to access the Internet network.

Connect your Raspberry Pi to the network through a UTP cable. In your network, make sure that there is a DHCP server because Raspberry Pi, by default, is configured as a DHCP client. This means Raspberry Pi will acquire an IP address:

After getting connected to a network, you can verify the IP address of Raspberry Pi. You can use the `ifconfig` command in a terminal to display the Raspberry Pi IP address:

```
$ ifconfig
```

Then, you should see the IP address of Raspberry Pi as follows:

```
● ● ●                    ⬆ agusk — pi@raspberrypi: ~ — ssh — 80×17
pi@raspberrypi ~ $ ifconfig
eth0      Link encap:Ethernet  HWaddr b8:27:eb:31:4e:cf
          inet addr:192.168.0.22  Bcast:192.168.0.255  Mask:255.255.255.0
          UP BROADCAST RUNNING MULTICAST  MTU:1500  Metric:1
          RX packets:5450 errors:0 dropped:0 overruns:0 frame:0
          TX packets:3477 errors:0 dropped:0 overruns:0 carrier:0
          collisions:0 txqueuelen:1000
          RX bytes:7470516 (7.1 MiB)  TX bytes:323713 (316.1 KiB)

lo        Link encap:Local Loopback
          inet addr:127.0.0.1  Mask:255.0.0.0
          UP LOOPBACK RUNNING  MTU:65536  Metric:1
          RX packets:8 errors:0 dropped:0 overruns:0 frame:0
          TX packets:8 errors:0 dropped:0 overruns:0 carrier:0
          collisions:0 txqueuelen:0
          RX bytes:1104 (1.0 KiB)  TX bytes:1104 (1.0 KiB)
```

If you want to change Raspberry Pi's IP address with a static IP address, you can modify the /etc/network/interfaces file. Open this file, for instance, and use nano:

```
$ sudo nano /etc/network/interfaces
```

Change dhcp to a static value to configure the static IP address on Raspberry Pi. For instance, you want to set the IP address 192.168.1.10 to Raspberry Pi. The following is the complete script of the /etc/network/interfaces file:

```
iface eth0 inet static
address 192.168.1.10
netmask 255.255.255.0
gateway 192.168.1.1
```

```
● ● ●                    ⬆ agusk — pi@raspberrypi: ~ — ssh — 80×17
pi@raspberrypi ~ $ ping packtpub.com
PING packtpub.com (83.166.169.231) 56(84) bytes of data.
64 bytes from 83.166.169.231: icmp_req=1 ttl=43 time=352 ms
64 bytes from 83.166.169.231: icmp_req=2 ttl=41 time=341 ms
64 bytes from 83.166.169.231: icmp_req=3 ttl=43 time=341 ms
64 bytes from 83.166.169.231: icmp_req=5 ttl=41 time=366 ms
64 bytes from 83.166.169.231: icmp_req=6 ttl=41 time=347 ms
64 bytes from 83.166.169.231: icmp_req=7 ttl=41 time=359 ms
64 bytes from 83.166.169.231: icmp_req=8 ttl=43 time=343 ms
64 bytes from 83.166.169.231: icmp_req=9 ttl=41 time=349 ms
64 bytes from 83.166.169.231: icmp_req=10 ttl=43 time=367 ms
64 bytes from 83.166.169.231: icmp_req=11 ttl=41 time=346 ms
64 bytes from 83.166.169.231: icmp_req=12 ttl=41 time=347 ms
```

Connecting to a wireless network

Raspberry Pi can be connected to a Wi-Fi network by attaching a Wi-Fi USB. The official Wi-Fi USB can be obtained from https://www.raspberrypi.org/products/usb-wifi-dongle/. You can also use another Wi-Fi USB from third-party vendors at your local electronics stores. The following is a list of Wi-Fi USBs for Raspberry Pi:

- The Wi-Fi USB module for Raspberry Pi, http://www.adafruit.com/products/1012

- The miniature Wi-Fi USB module for Raspberry Pi, http://www.adafruit.com/products/2638

Let's start by attaching the Wi-Fi USB into a Raspberry Pi board. We can use the Wi-Fi USB from Belkin. This tool is recognized by the Raspbian OS:

We can connect to a hotspot via a GUI and a command line. If you're working on a Raspbian desktop, you should see a Wi-Fi configuration tool in **Menu — Preferences**. Open **WiFi Configuration,** so you can see this tool form, as shown in the following figure:

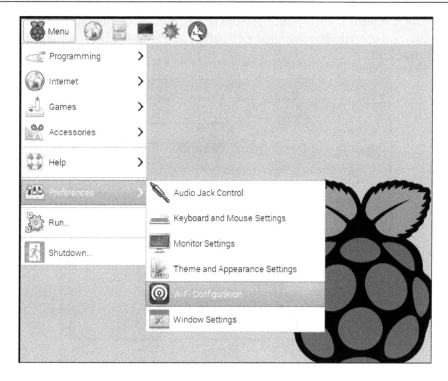

To select a hotspot, you click the **Scan** button. Then, there is a list of SSIDs. Select your SSID and fill in the SSID key. Click the **Scan** button. Then, select the preferred SSID:

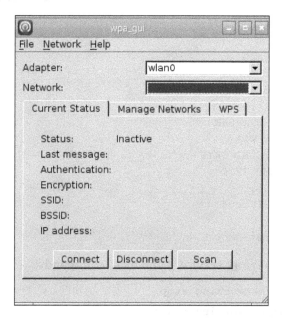

After getting connected, you should see the IP address of Raspberry Pi, for instance, `192.168.0.28`. To verify the installed network, you can use a browser and navigate to a particular URL:

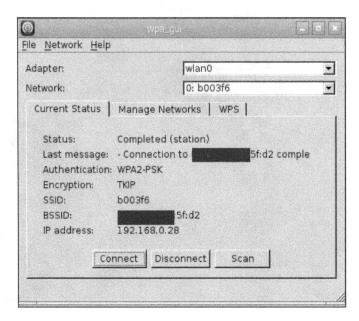

We can set a specific SSID by modifying the `/etc/network/interfaces` file. For instance, your Raspberry Pi connects to MySSID with key MySSIDKey. Add the following scripts:

```
auto wlan0
allow-hotplug wlan0
iface wlan0 inet dhcp
    wpa-scan-ssid 1
    wpa-ap-scan 1
    wpa-key-mgmt WPA-PSK
    wpa-proto RSN WPA
    wpa-pairwise CCMP TKIP
    wpa-group CCMP TKIP
    wpa-ssid "MySSID"
    wpa-psk "MySSIDKey"

iface default inet dhcp
```

Save and restart the network service. Type these commands:

```
$ sudo /etc/init.d/networking stop
$ sudo /etc/init.d/networking start
```

You can also reboot Raspberry Pi if you obtain an error. Just type the following command to restart Raspberry Pi:

```
$ sudo reboot
```

To verify your Internet network, you can do ping or open a browser that is navigated to a specific URL:

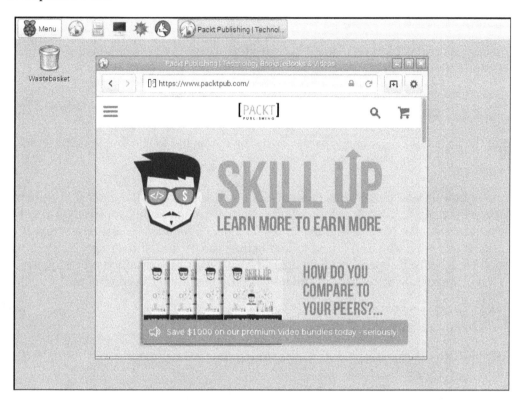

Introducing Node.js

Node.js is used to build a network and a server-side application. We can also build web applications using Node.js. In this section, I will introduce you to how to use Node.js on Raspberry Pi. Then, use it to control sensor or actuator devices. The last task is to show how to publish sensor or actuator to be controlled via a browser or a mobile Android application. For further information about Node.js, you can visit the official Node.js website at http://www.nodejs.org.

To install Node.js runtime on Raspberry Pi, assuming that you use Raspbian OS, you can type the following commands in the terminal:

```
$ sudo apt-get update
$ sudo apt-get install nodejs
```

To verify the Node.js program, you can type the following command:

```
$ nodejs -v
```

You can also install Node.js using Adafruit's Raspberry Pi package repository. Type the following commands:

```
$ curl -sLS https://apt.adafruit.com/add | sudo bash
$ sudo apt-get install node
```

After the installation, you can type the following command to check a Node program:

```
$ node -v
```

Those methods take the older version of Node.js. You can install the latest version of Node.js by compiling Node.js source code. The advantage of this approach is to get the latest version of Node.js and minimize the library dependencies. I recommend you do it this way. You don't need to do the first and second of the previous tasks to install Node.js from source code. By default, GCC is already installed on Raspberry Pi. If it is not installed, you can install it by typing the following commands:

```
$ sudo apt-get update
$ sudo apt-get install build-essential
```

Now you can download and extract the source code file using the following commands:

```
$ wget http://nodejs.org/dist/node-latest.tar.gz
$ tar -xzf node-latest.tar.gz
```

You should see a folder node-vX.Y.Z where X.Y.Z is a Node.js version. For instance, I have node-v0.12.7. Then, type the following commands to install Node.js from the source code:

```
$ ls
$ cd node-v0.12.7
$ ./configure
$ make
$ sudo make install
```

The compiling process takes a long time. After finishing the installation, you can verify using the node -v command:

```
● ● ●        ⬆ agusk — pi@raspberrypi: ~/src/node-v0.12.7 — ssh — 80×15
installing /usr/local/include/node/openssl/opensslconf.h
installing /usr/local/include/node/v8-profiler.h
installing /usr/local/include/node/v8config.h
installing /usr/local/include/node/v8.h
installing /usr/local/include/node/v8-debug.h
installing /usr/local/include/node/v8stdint.h
installing /usr/local/include/node/v8-testing.h
installing /usr/local/include/node/v8-util.h
installing /usr/local/include/node/v8-platform.h
installing /usr/local/include/node/libplatform/libplatform.h
installing /usr/local/include/node/zconf.h
installing /usr/local/include/node/zlib.h
pi@raspberrypi ~/src/node-v0.12.7 $ node -v
v0.12.7
pi@raspberrypi ~/src/node-v0.12.7 $
```

To test our Node.js program, you can write a simple Node.js app, Hello World. Create a file named hello.js and write the following script:

```
// hello.js
console.log("Hello Node.js");
```

Save this file. Then, you can run this file using the node or nodejs command:

```
$ node hello.js
```

You should see the program output, which displays **Hello Node.js**:

```
● ● ●          ⬆ agusk — pi@raspberrypi: ~/led/ch7 — ssh — 80×7
pi@raspberrypi ~/led/ch7 $ node hello.js
Hello Node.js
pi@raspberrypi ~/led/ch7 $
```

Controlling LEDs and lamps using Node.js

In some previous chapters, we learned how to control sensor or actuator devices using Python. In this section, I will show you how to build a program using Node.js to control simple actuator devices, such as LEDs. There are many Node.js libraries, which are able to access Raspberry Pi GPIO. One of these libraries is `rpi-gpio`. You can find it at `https://www.npmjs.com/package/rpi-gpio`.

You can install `rpi-gpio` using the `npm` command:

```
$ npm install rpi-gpio
```

Your Raspberry Pi must be connected to an Internet network because Pi needs to download this module.

Another approach is that you can define your module dependencies on the `package.json` file. Just write this script into a file named `package.json`:

```
{
  "name": "chapter7",
  "version": "0.0.1",
  "dependencies":{
    "rpi-gpio": "latest",
    "async": "latest"


  }
}
```

After that, you can install Node.js modules from the `package.json` file by typing the following command:

```
$ npm install
```

```
● ● ●          ⬆ agusk — pi@raspberrypi: ~/led/ch7 — ssh — 80×10
  COPY Release/epoll.node
make: Leaving directory '/home/pi/led/ch7/node_modules/rpi-gpio/node_modules/epo
ll/build'
async@1.4.2 node_modules/async

rpi-gpio@0.6.0 node_modules/rpi-gpio
├── debug@0.8.1
├── async@0.8.0
└── epoll@0.1.13 (bindings@1.2.1, nan@1.8.4)
pi@raspberrypi ~/led/ch7 $ ▌
```

To use the `rpi-gpio` library, we will try to build a simple program, blinking.
We need three LEDs, which are attached to Raspberry Pi GPIO. In this scenario,
we're going to turn on/off these LEDs. The following is the hardware wiring:

- LED 1 is connected to Raspberry Pi *GPIO0* (physical 11, BCM=17)
- LED 2 is connected to Raspberry Pi *GPIO2* (physical 13, BCM=27)
- LED 3 is connected to Raspberry Pi *GPIO3* (physical 15, BCM=22)

You can see my wiring implementation, as shown in the following figure:

The `rpi-gpio` library defines the GPIO pin using BCM and Pi. By default, this
library uses Pi GPIO. You can see Raspberry Pi GPIO using `gpio readall` (please
read *Chapter 1, Getting started with LED programming through Raspberry Pi GPIO*).
Since Node.js runs asynchronously, we can use the `async` library to run Node.js
synchronously. Type the following command to install `async`:

```
$ npm install async
```

We need the `async` module because Node.js runs single threads and leverages asynchronous calls. The `async` module can be used to make sure that our tasks run sequentially; for instance, write data into GPIO after opening GPIO. You can read further information about the `async` module at `https://github.com/caolan/async`.

Now, let's start to build our program. Create a file named `blinking.js` and write the complete code as follows:

```
// blinking.js
var gpio = require('rpi-gpio');
var async = require('async');

async.parallel([
    function(callback) {
        gpio.setup(11, gpio.DIR_OUT, callback)
    },
    function(callback) {
        gpio.setup(13, gpio.DIR_OUT, callback)
    },
    function(callback) {
        gpio.setup(15, gpio.DIR_OUT, callback)
    }
], function(err, results) {
    console.log('Pins set up');
    write();
});

function write() {
    async.series([
        function(callback) {
            delayedWrite(11, true, callback);
        },
        function(callback) {
            delayedWrite(13, true, callback);
        },
        function(callback) {
            delayedWrite(15, true, callback);
        },
        function(callback) {
            delayedWrite(11, false, callback);
        },
        function(callback) {
            delayedWrite(13, false, callback);
        },
```

```
            function(callback) {
                delayedWrite(15, false, callback);
            }
        ], function(err, results) {
            console.log('Writes complete, pause then unexport pins');
            setTimeout(function() {
                gpio.destroy(function() {
                    console.log('Closed pins, now exit');
                });
            }, 500);
        });
    }

    function delayedWrite(pin, value, callback) {
        setTimeout(function() {
            gpio.write(pin, value, callback);
        }, 500);
    }
```

Save this code.

The explanation is as follows:

- First, we define our pin mode using gpio.setup() as DIR_OUT for all LEDs.
- To turn on the LED, we call gpio.write() by passing true, and to turn it off, we pass false.
- The delay process can be used to hold a specific task, for instance, hold lighting LED for about 500 ms. To simulate delay() in our program, we can use setTimeout() about 500 ms. The setTimeout() function has already been available in JavaScript.
- gpio.destroy() is used to release all usage resources.

Since the program accesses hardware, you should use sudo while running the program. Type the following command to run the program:

```
$ sudo node blinking.js
```

This program will turn on LED 1, 2, and 3. After this, the program will turn off all LEDs sequentially. You can see the sample of lighting LED and the program output.

A sample output from a program can be seen in the following figure:

```
● ● ●            ⬆ agusk — pi@raspberrypi: ~/led/ch7 — ssh — 80×10
pi@raspberrypi ~/led/ch7 $ sudo node blinking.js
Pins set up
Writes complete, pause then unexport pins
Closed pins, now exit
pi@raspberrypi ~/led/ch7 $ ▓
```

Three LEDs are lit sequentially. A sample output of lit LEDs can be seen in the following figure:

Building a simple web server using Node.js

As I stated, Node.js can be used to build a web application. We can use the HTTP library to build a simple web server. Let's try to write the following code:

```
var http = require('http');

http.createServer(function (req, res) {
    res.writeHead(200, {'Content-Type': 'text/plain'});
    res.end('Hello Node.js');
}).listen(8056);
console.log('Server running at port 8056');
```

Save this code into a file named `mywebserver.js`. The `http.createServer()` function is used to create a web server with a specific port. In this case, I used port *8056*.

Now you can run this file. Type the following command:

$ node mywebserver.js

To test this program, open a browser and navigate to `http://<ip_address_raspberry_pi>:8056`. You should see **Hello Node.js** in your browser as follows:

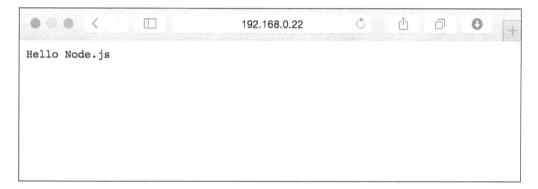

Building RESTful using Node.js

After creating a simple web server, we can build a simple RESTful. **REST** stands for **Representational State Transfer**. It uses primitive HTTP operations to maintain communication between the server and the client. In this section, I implement RESTful using **Express** for Node.js. This library can cut your development time to build a web application.

For further information about Express, please visit `http://expressjs.com`. We also need **body-parser** to work with JSON data. **JSON (JavaScript Object Notation)** is a lightweight data-interchange format and easy to read and write. The following is a sample of JSON data:

```
{
    name: 'foo',
    email: 'foo@email.com',
    leve: 3
}
```

We are going to use JSON to exchange data between the server and the client.

To install Express and body-parser, you can use `npm`. Type the following commands:

```
$ npm install express
$ npm install body-parser
```

For testing, we build a simple RESTful app, which serves HTTP GET JSON. Create a file named `myrest.js` and write the complete code as follows:

```
// myrest.js
var express = require('express');
var app = express();
var bodyParser = require('body-parser');
var port = 8099;

app.use(bodyParser.urlencoded({ extended: false }));
app.use(bodyParser.json());

app.get('/', function (req, res) {
    var data ={
        status:"ok",
        msg: "hello world"
    };
    res.json(data);
});

app.listen(port);
console.log('Server was started on ' + port);
```

This program will run on port *8099*. To run the program, you can type the following command:

```
$ node myrest.js
```

Then, open your browser and navigate to `http://<ip_address_of_app>:8099/`. You should see the JSON data from the server:

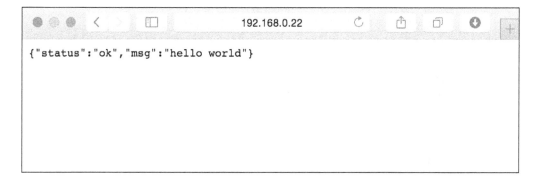

Controlling LEDs through RESTful

After learning to build a RESTful app, we continue to control sensor or actuator devices from RESTful. For instance, we want to turn on an LED by calling `http://<server>/led1`. In this case, Express receives HTTP GET from client. If the request is `/led1`, Express will turn on the LED for a certain time and then turn it off.

To implement this scenario, let's start to build a program. Create a file named `ledrest.js` and write the following complete code:

```
// ledrest.js
var gpio = require('rpi-gpio');
var express = require('express');
var app = express();
var bodyParser = require('body-parser');
var port = 8099;


app.use(bodyParser.urlencoded({ extended: false }));
app.use(bodyParser.json());

gpio.setup(11, gpio.DIR_OUT);
gpio.setup(13, gpio.DIR_OUT);
gpio.setup(15, gpio.DIR_OUT);

function off1() {
    setTimeout(function() {
        gpio.write(11, 0);
    }, 2000);
```

```
}
function off2() {
    setTimeout(function() {
        gpio.write(13, 0);
    }, 2000);
}
function off3() {
    setTimeout(function() {
        gpio.write(15, 0);
    }, 2000);
}

function run_led1() {
    setTimeout(function() {
        console.log('led1 is on');
        gpio.write(11, 1, off1);

    }, 2000);
}
function run_led2() {
    setTimeout(function() {
        console.log('led2 is on');
        gpio.write(13, 1, off2);

    }, 2000);
}
function run_led3() {
    setTimeout(function() {
        console.log('led3 is on');
        gpio.write(15, 1, off3);

    }, 2000);
}

app.get('/led1', function (req, res) {
    run_led1();

    var data ={status:"ok",led:1};
    res.json(data);
});
app.get('/led2', function (req, res) {
    run_led2();

    var data ={status:"ok",led:2};
```

```
        res.json(data);
    });
app.get('/led3', function (req, res) {
        run_led3();

        var data ={status:"ok",led:3};
        res.json(data);
    });

    app.listen(port);
    console.log('Server was started on ' + port);
```

We use the same hardware wiring from the previous section, which involved three LEDs. The LEDs are connected to *GPIO0, GPIO2,* and *GPIO3.*

Save this file. Run the program by typing the following command:

```
$ sudo node ledrest.js
```

To test the program, open a browser. For instance, we want to turn on/off LED 1, so you navigate the browser to http://<server>:port/led1 . After navigating to http://<server>:port/led1, you should see LED 1 is lit and then it's off. Try to test LED 2 and 3. A sample output for a lit LED and program output can be seen in the following figure:

You should also see a response from the server on your browser. A sample output from the browser can be seen in the following figure:

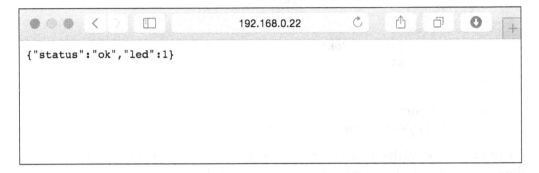

Building a PhoneGap application for Android

In this section, we will build an Android application using PhoneGap. This development is performed on your local computer.

PhoneGap is a tool to build a cross-platform mobile app using web technologies, such as HTML5, JS, and Angular. This tool can cut down your mobile development time. Once you have created the PhoneGap app, you can compile it to Android, iOS, Windows Phone, and Blackberry. Please visit http://phonegap.com to get more information about PhoneGap.

In this section, I only share how to build a PhoneGap app for an Android platform target. The following are required libraries for PhoneGap:

- Java JDK, http://www.oracle.com/technetwork/java/javase/downloads/index.html
- Android SDK, https://developer.android.com/sdk/index.html
- Ant, http://ant.apache.org
- Node.js, http://www.nodejs.org

You need to install an Android API, for instance, Android 4.0.x, Android Kitkat 4.4, and Android simulator. These are used for development. Configuring an Android simulator can be managed using AVD Android.

Please configure your AVD Android to create an Android emulator, so you don't need the real hardware to run an Android app. For testing, I used Android API 19 with Android 4.4.2:

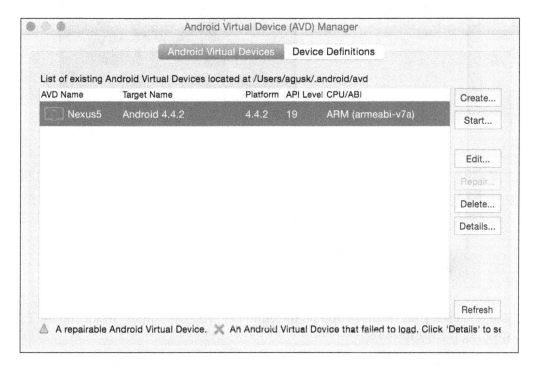

You can install PhoneGap via Node.js. Type the following command:

```
$ sudo npm install -g phonegap
```

After it is installed, you can verify PhoneGap by checking its version:

```
$ phonegap -v
```

You should see the PhoneGap version.

Now, let's build the first PhoneGap Android app. To create PhoneGap, your computer must be connected to the Internet network because it will download a project template.

Type the following commands:

```
$ phonegap create hello-android
$ cd hello-android
$ phonegap build android
$ phonegap run android --emulator
```

Boom! You should see the Android emulator as follows:

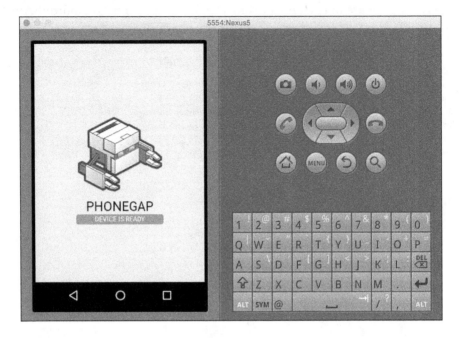

If you don't see your Android app on the emulator, you can run the following by displaying the log message:

```
$ phonegap run android --emulator --verbose
```

The following is a list of recommendation you take to fix your problem:

- Add the `icon.png` file into the root folder of your project
- Change the minimum SDK version, for instance, 19, `<preference name="android-minSdkVersion" value="19" />` on the `config.xml` file and `<uses-sdk android:minSdkVersion="19" android:targetSdkVersion="22" />` on the `AndroidManifest.xml` file

Connecting PhoneGap Android to Raspberry Pi through RESTful

It's more convenient to control three LEDs from the Android app. It's fine if you use a browser on Android and navigate to the RESTful server on Raspberry Pi. We call our RESTful from the Android app. In this section, we will build a PhoneGap app for the Android target and control the three LEDs. We use the previous program, the `ledrest.js` file, as a RESTful server, which controls LEDs on Raspberry Pi.

First, we create a PhoneGap project named `leds-android`:

```
$ phonegap create leds-android
$ cd /leds-android
$ phonegap build android --verbose
```

Try to run the program on the Android emulator for testing purposes:

```
$ phonegap run android --emulator --verbose
```

If the program runs well, we continue to modify our program. To communicate between the PhoneGap Android and RESTful server, we use jQuery, the https://jquery.com. Place `jquery-*.*.*.min.js` file into the `<project_root>/www/js` folder. The next step is to modify the `index.html` and `index.js` files:

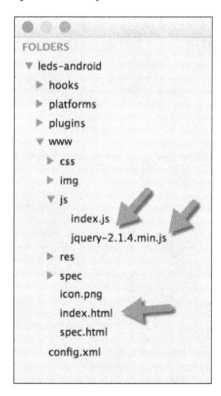

Basically, we add the jQuery file into `index.html`. Then, we add three buttons: LED 1, LED 2, and LED 3. A click event on these buttons is implemented in the `index.js` file. The following are the complete script for the `index.html` file:

```html
<!DOCTYPE html>
<html>
    <head>
        <meta charset="utf-8" />
        <meta name="format-detection" content="telephone=no" />
        <meta name="msapplication-tap-highlight" content="no" />
        <!-- WARNING: for iOS 7, remove the width=device-width and
height=device-height attributes. See https://issues.apache.org/jira/
browse/CB-4323 -->
        <meta name="viewport" content="user-scalable=no, initial-
scale=1, maximum-scale=1, minimum-scale=1, width=device-width,
height=device-height, target-densitydpi=device-dpi" />
        <link rel="stylesheet" type="text/css" href="css/index.css" />
        <title>Hello World</title>
    </head>
    <body>
        <div class="app">
            <h1>PhoneGap</h1>
            <div>
                <input type="button" id="led1" value="LED 1">
            </div>
            <div>
                <input type="button" id="led2" value="LED 2">
            </div>
            <div>
                <input type="button" id="led3" value="LED 3">
            </div>
        </div>
        <script type="text/javascript" src="cordova.js"></script>
        <script type="text/javascript" src="js/jquery-
2.1.4.min.js"></script>
        <script type="text/javascript" src="js/index.js"></script>
        <script type="text/javascript">
            app.initialize();
        </script>
    </body>
</html>
```

Now modify the index.js file. In this file, we add a click event for three buttons. To call RESTful from PhoneGap, we use $.ajax() from jQuery. Please change the IP address of Raspberry Pi. The following is the complete scripts for the index.js file.

```
var app = {
    initialize: function() {
        this.bindEvents();
    },
    bindEvents: function() {
        document.addEventListener('deviceready', this.onDeviceReady,
false);
    },
    onDeviceReady: function() {
        app.receivedEvent('deviceready');
    },
    receivedEvent: function(id) {
        $("#led1").click(function(){
            $.ajax({
                url : 'http://192.168.0.22:8099/led1',
                type : 'GET',
                dataType : 'JSON',
                crossDomain: true,
                success : function(data) {
                    alert(data.status);
                },
                error : function() {}
            });
        });
        $("#led2").click(function(){
            $.ajax({
                url : 'http://192.168.0.22:8099/led2',
                type : 'GET',
                dataType : 'JSON',
                crossDomain: true,
                success : function(data) {
                    alert(data.status);
                },
                error : function() {}
            });
        });
        $("#led3").click(function(){
            $.ajax({
                url : 'http://192.168.0.22:8099/led3',
                type : 'GET',
```

```
                    dataType : 'JSON',
                    crossDomain: true,
                    success : function(data) {
                        alert(data.status);
                    },
                    error : function() {}
                });
            });
        }
    };
```

Save all files.

You can build and run this program into the emulator:

```
$ phonegap build android --verbose
$ phonegap run android --emulator --verbose
```

After the program is loaded into the emulator, you should see three buttons. Click on **LED 1** to turn on LED 1 at a certain time. Test again by clicking on **LED 2** and **LED 3** too. You should get the **ok** response from the server:

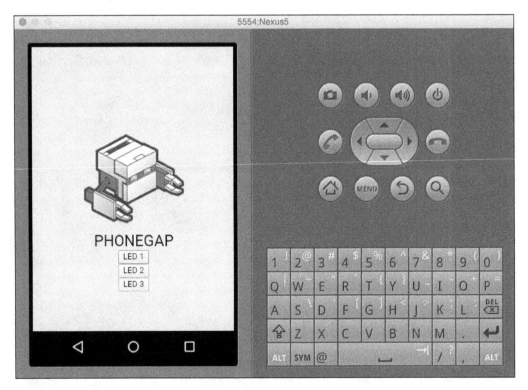

After your program is running, you can click on **LED 1, 2,** or **3** buttons to turn on the LEDs. You should also see a notification dialog from the program, as shown in the following figure:

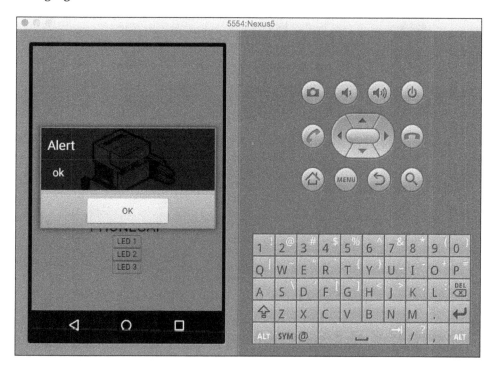

Summary

We learned how to control a sensor or an actuator; for testing, we used LEDs, from an Android app through RESTful. We built RESTful using Node.js and Express. For more practices, you can build your own home automation, which can be controlled from the Internet network.

By combining your experience from all the chapters, you can build applications by utilizing a module based-LED on Raspberry Pi. We can control our program via either a wired or wireless network, such as Wi-Fi and Bluetooth. This means that you learned how to build an IoT application for Raspberry Pi.

Index

wired network, connecting to 130, 131
wireless network, connecting to 132-135

D

digital clock
  4-digit 7-segment display 47-49
  building, I2C OLED graphic
      display used 57-59

E

Express
  URL 144

G

General-purpose input/output (GPIO) 4

I

I2C (Inter-IC) bus 50
I2C OLED graphic display
  about 49, 50
  characters, displaying 54-56
  I2C, enabling on Raspberry Pi 50-53
  I2C library for Python 53
  numbers, displaying 54-56
  used, for building digital clock 57-59
iBeacon
  about 112
  building, on Bluetooth 4 (BLE)
      stack 112-114
IC MAX7219
  reference 63, 64
IC MCP23017
  about 87
  reference 88
integrated circuits (ICs) 50
Intellij IDEA
  URL 116
Internet network 129

J

JSON (JavaScript Object Notation) 144

L

lamps
  controlling, Node.js used 138-142
LED
  controlling, Node.js used 138-142
  controlling, through RESTful 145-148
  turning on/off, through push button 11-14
LED blinking 7-10
LED dot matrix display
  about 61-64
  online electronics stores 63
  random character, displaying 70-72
  random number, displaying 68-70
LED dot matrix driver
  about 64
  matrix 7219 driver, deploying 66-68
  Raspberry Pi SPI, enabling 65, 66
LED dot matrix modules
  cascading 75-78

M

master 64
Master reset (MR) 30
matrix 7219 driver
  deploying 66-68
  reference 66
microcontroller (MCU) 28

N

Node.js
  about 135
  installing 136
  program, testing 137
  URL 135
  used, for building RESTful 143, 144
  used, for building simple web server 143
  used, for controlling LEDs
      and lamps 138-142

O

OLED (organic light-emitting diode) 49

Thank you for buying
Raspberry Pi LED Blueprints

About Packt Publishing

Packt, pronounced 'packed', published its first book, *Mastering phpMyAdmin for Effective MySQL Management*, in April 2004, and subsequently continued to specialize in publishing highly focused books on specific technologies and solutions.

Our books and publications share the experiences of your fellow IT professionals in adapting and customizing today's systems, applications, and frameworks. Our solution-based books give you the knowledge and power to customize the software and technologies you're using to get the job done. Packt books are more specific and less general than the IT books you have seen in the past. Our unique business model allows us to bring you more focused information, giving you more of what you need to know, and less of what you don't.

Packt is a modern yet unique publishing company that focuses on producing quality, cutting-edge books for communities of developers, administrators, and newbies alike. For more information, please visit our website at www.packtpub.com.

About Packt Open Source

In 2010, Packt launched two new brands, Packt Open Source and Packt Enterprise, in order to continue its focus on specialization. This book is part of the Packt Open Source brand, home to books published on software built around open source licenses, and offering information to anybody from advanced developers to budding web designers. The Open Source brand also runs Packt's Open Source Royalty Scheme, by which Packt gives a royalty to each open source project about whose software a book is sold.

Writing for Packt

We welcome all inquiries from people who are interested in authoring. Book proposals should be sent to author@packtpub.com. If your book idea is still at an early stage and you would like to discuss it first before writing a formal book proposal, then please contact us; one of our commissioning editors will get in touch with you.

We're not just looking for published authors; if you have strong technical skills but no writing experience, our experienced editors can help you develop a writing career, or simply get some additional reward for your expertise.

Raspberry Pi Blueprints

ISBN: 978-1-78439-290-1   Paperback: 284 pages

Design and build your own hardware projects that interact with the real world using the Raspberry Pi

1. Interact with a wide range of additional sensors and devices via Raspberry Pi.

2. Create exciting, low-cost products ranging from radios to home security and weather systems.

3. Full of simple, easy-to-understand instructions to create projects that even have professional-quality enclosures.

Raspberry Pi Super Cluster

ISBN: 978-1-78328-619-5   Paperback: 126 pages

Build your own parallel-computing cluster using Raspberry Pi in the comfort of your home

1. Learn about parallel computing by building your own system using Raspberry Pi.

2. Build a two-node parallel computing cluster.

3. Integrate Raspberry Pi with Hadoop to build your own super cluster.

Please check **www.PacktPub.com** for information on our titles

Learning Raspberry Pi

ISBN: 978-1-78398-282-0   Paperback: 258 pages

Unlock your creative programming potential by creating web technologies, image processing, electronics- and robotics-based projects using the Raspberry Pi

1. Learn how to create games, web, and desktop applications using the best features of the Raspberry Pi.

2. Discover the powerful development tools that allow you to cross-compile your software and build your own Linux distribution for maximum performance.

3. Step-by-step tutorials show you how to quickly develop real-world applications using the Raspberry Pi.

Raspberry Pi Robotic Projects

ISBN: 978-1-84969-432-2   Paperback: 278 pages

Create amazing robotic projects on a shoestring budget

1. Make your projects talk and understand speech with Raspberry Pi.

2. Use standard webcam to make your projects see and enhance vision capabilities.

3. Full of simple, easy-to-understand instructions to bring your Raspberry Pi online for developing robotics projects.

Please check **www.PacktPub.com** for information on our titles